THE FRENCH ARE IN THE BAY
THE EXPEDITION TO BANTRY BAY, 1796

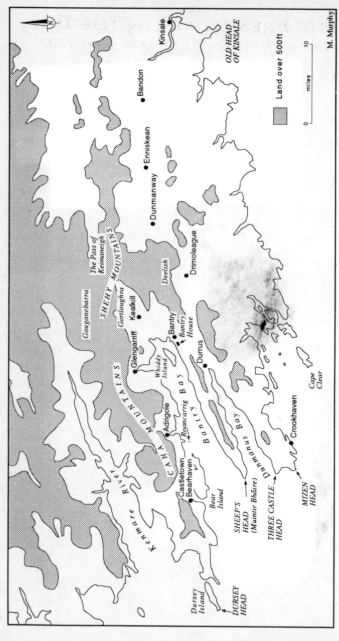

West Cork: Placenames mentioned in the book

M. Murphy

THE FRENCH ARE IN THE BAY

THE EXPEDITION TO BANTRY BAY, 1796

Oh, The French are in the Bay
They'll be here without delay
And the Orange will decay
Says the Sean Bhean Bhocht
Traditional Ballad

Edited by

JOHN A. MURPHY

MERCIER PRESS

MERCIER PRESS
PO Box 5, 5 French Church Street, Cork
and
16 Hume Street, Dublin

Trade enquiries to CMD DISTRIBUTION,
55a Spruce Avenue, Stillorgan Industrial Park, Blackrock, Dublin

© Contributors, 1997

ISBN 1 85635 171 8

10 9 8 7 6 5 4 3 2 1

A CIP record for this book is available from the British Library.

Printed in Ireland by Colour Books Ltd.

CONTENTS

This book is dedicated to
JENNIE MCCARTHY AND SEÁN KELLY

INTRODUCTION

This book is based on the lectures given at the Bantry Bay Summer School in July 1996. The School was one of a number of events marking the bicentenary of the French expeditionary armada which arrived off Bantry Bay in December 1796. That expedition seemed to be the fulfilment of the aspirations of Theobald Wolfe Tone and his United Irishmen colleagues who had long looked to revolutionary France to help 'break the connection with England' and establish an Irish Republic based on a brotherhood of all Irishmen and on the Rights of Man.

In the event, the great enterprise was dogged by disaster, not least by the vagaries of the winter weather, so that a landing never took place and the badly scattered fleet limped back to France. But Tone noted that 'England has not had such an escape since the Spanish Armada' and a modern historian has written: 'It had been a close call but England survives on close calls'.

Bantry Bay had been chosen by the leaders of the expedition because of its fine harbour, its relative proximity to France (normally less than two days sail from Brest) and its ready access to Cork, the prosperous second city of the kingdom and the major victualling depot for the British navy. Historians today would generally concur with W. E. H. Lecky's judgement that if the French had landed at Bantry, Cork would have been taken with relative ease and a nation-wide rebellion might well have ensued.

In the bicentenary year of the expedition, modern Bantry was very much aware of this aspect of its heritage. Wolfe Tone, the dominant personality of the 1796 event who has left us such a vivid first hand account of the expedition, is well commemorated in the town. He would have been greatly pleased at having a public house as well as a street named after him! Overlooking the scenic Bantry Bay, in the east stables of the splendid Bantry House, a permanent French Armada Exhibition graphically presents the story of the abortive mission. The location of the exhibition is nicely ironic, since Richard White, the proprietor of Bantry House (or Seafield House as it then was) in 1796 was made Lord Bantry for his vigilance and loyalty during the French scare, and was thus enabled to put the family fortunes on a secure foundation.

The failure of the French to land does not diminish the fascination of the event for scholars, nor detract from its historical significance. In this book, as at the School itself, leading scholars investigate and analyse various aspects of the epic enterprise – the revolutionary background and the French strategy behind the expedition; the role of Wolfe Tone; the British and Irish military and naval contexts; popular beliefs and expectations; the perspective of political balladry; the Bantry dimension; the wider social and political frameworks; and, not least, the role of the weather in political destiny. After all, the Bantry Bay expedition could have changed the history of these islands, weather permitting!

As Chairman of the 1996 Bantry Bay Summer School, and editor of this book, my thanks are due in the first place to the Bantry Bay '96 Committee (chaired by Matt Murphy) and the various sponsors for their initiative and generosity in funding the Summer School, out of which this book grew. As a non-playing captain, so to speak, I am indebted to the individual writers here, both for their enthusiastic participation in the School and their ready co-operation in the preparation of the book for publication. I am happy that the appearance of this work continues Mercier's long and honourable association with Irish scholarship.

Finally, the contributors join with me in expressing our appreciation of the enthusiastic labours of the two local organisers of the Bantry Bay Summer School, Jennie McCarthy and Seán Kelly, to whom the book is dedicated.

John A. Murphy
University College, Cork
February, 1997

ANATOMY OF A FAILURE
BANTRY BAY AND THE FRENCH INVASION OF 1796

Hugh Gough

The French were on the sea in numbers in the winter of 1796. On 16 December a fleet of 48 ships under the command of vice-admiral Morard de Galles left Brest with over 13,000 experienced troops on board, bound for Bantry Bay under the command of one of France's most charismatic generals, Lazare Hoche. There they were to land, link up with local insurgents and capture Cork before the end of the month. From there Hoche was to march on Dublin, convoke an Irish Convention to draw up a republican constitution for the country, and prepare for an invasion of England. The plan was ambitious, but not over-ambitious when compared with the victories that French armies had already achieved elsewhere in western Europe, and if it had succeeded it would certainly have changed the course of European history. The revolutionary wars would probably have ended as Britain sued for peace, France would have been left in control of most of western Europe and the military crisis that brought Napoleon Bonaparte to power three years later might never have happened. Ireland, for its part, would have become a republic, with debts to repay to the French for the cost of Hoche's army, and close trading links. Yet the expedition was a failure and in the early days of 1797 the remnants of the fleet began straggling home to Brest in disarray after two weeks at sea without landing a single soldier on Irish soil. Against the odds, Britain survived to carry on the fight against France for another eighteen years and Ireland's integration with Britain was tightened still further four years later with the passing of the Act of Union. Why did the French risk such large troop numbers on an invasion of Ireland in the middle of winter? What were they hoping to achieve, why did they fail and what would have happened in Ireland if the expedition had been successful? This paper only attempts to give a partial answer to these questions, concentrating on the French side of the affair and leaving the potential consequences of a successful invasion to other contributors. Yet, in doing so, it attempts to throw light on the aims and ambitions behind a fated expedition which left a sunken warship, the *Surveillante*, behind in Bantry Bay and over 1,500 French soldiers and sailors in watery graves in the Atlantic Ocean between Bantry and the Brittany coast.

When revolution broke out in France in 1789, most European governments were happy enough to see one of Europe's most powerful countries diverted from international power politics into the complicated process of domestic reform. Revolutionary politicians in France shared that pleasure, arguing that wars were the work of ambitious kings rather than of free people, and proclaiming in May 1790 that France would live at peace with its neighbours, renouncing the idea of undertaking any offensive war. Yet the promise proved short-lived, for within two years a group of radicals, the Girondins, seized the political initiative by arguing that war offered a solution to the growing problems posed to the revolution by political division, religious schism and counter-revolution. France duly declared war on Austria in April 1792 and the Girondins quickly expanded the conflict into a European crusade, proclaiming that French armies would assist people anywhere wanting to rid themselves of tyranny. By the summer of 1793 this virtual declaration of war on the European state system had prompted the formation by the British Prime Minister, William Pitt, of the First Coalition to combat France. Its initial victories toppled the Girondins, who were replaced by a Jacobin-led Committee of Public Safety which enforced a regime of terror to silence internal dissent and mould French armies into a formidable military machine. From the summer of 1794 onwards those armies took the offensive, annexing the Austrian Netherlands (modern Belgium), invading the United Provinces, occupying the German Rhineland, and absorbing Savoy and Nice. The First Coalition melted away and by the spring of 1796 a sizeable body of opinion within France favoured peace and a return to political normality. Yet Austria was unlikely to agree to the loss of Belgium and of the Rhineland states of the Holy Roman Empire, while Britain was implacably opposed to French expansion into Belgium and Holland.

In the autumn of 1795 a new political regime had come to power in France, the Directory, which placed executive power in the hands of five Directors and legislative power under the control of two elected Councils. The Directors planned a military offensive for the spring of 1796 which involved a three pronged attack on Austria, with two armies advancing through Germany and a third, under the newly appointed Napoleon Bonaparte, through northern Italy. Yet the Directory also retained the hope of mounting some kind of diversionary attack on England, to force Britain to sue for peace. Three years earlier, in the autumn of 1793, the Committee of Public Safety had ordered the mobilisation of 100,000 men on the coasts of Brittany and Normandy for just such an invasion. At the same time Hoche, then serving in the Army of the North, had urged the Committee of Public Safety to allow him to lead a smaller invasion force: 'A courageous man at the head of 40,000 others would cause a lot of damage in that country, and force the tyrants united against us to sue for peace ... I want to be the first to set foot on the land of these political brigands'.[1] Neither initiative had come to anything because there were no resources to spare, and even in the winter of 1795–6 the scale of the offensive against Austria ruled out the possibility of a serious invasion. Yet Lazare Carnot, the Director who masterminded military strategy and a former member of the Committee of Public Safety, was an anglophobe who wanted revenge on Britain for the role that she had played in supporting the guerrilla-based counter-revolution in the Vendée and Brittany since 1793. His attitude was shared by Hoche, who had commanded the army that pacified the area in 1795–6, and when Carnot contacted him about the logistics of a disruptive English invasion in April 1796, Hoche was immediately enthusiastic.[2]

Carnot's plan was to recruit some 2,000 convicts, equip them with a crude uniform and a range of basic weapons (essentially a double barrelled gun, two pistols, a knife and a supply of ammunition), then land them at various points in southern England.[3] They would then split up into small groups to attack government convoys, destroy town halls, blow up bridges and obstruct roads. The aim was to spread so much panic among the civilian population that Pitt would be forced to divert troops into civilian protection and sue for peace. The convicts would then return to France as free men, with permission to keep the profits of their activity, up to a value of 100,000 francs.[4] Hoche assured Carnot that he could find a thousand troublemakers from within his own army for the expedition, along with a further 1,200 prisoners, condemned to forced labour or life in the galleys for various disciplinary offences, to land in Wales as a supplementary force. However, this bizarre plan was rapidly overtaken by the idea of an Irish expedition, for in early February 1796 Wolfe Tone landed in Le Havre from America, intent on persuading the French to mount just such an invasion. His chances of success initially seemed slim, for the revolution had already burnt its fingers on the optimism of political exiles from the United Provinces, Belgium and the Rhineland states who, like Tone, had assured it that a French invasion would detonate a revolutionary uprising. In all these cases, when French armies had invaded, the vast majority of the population rejected their reforms and resented military occupation, so that by 1796 the France wanted proof of revolutionary commitment before she was prepared to risk troops and money in an act of political liberation. The Irish had not been particularly active among exile groups earlier in the revolution, so when Tone initially argued his case at the Department of Foreign Affairs during mid-February 1796, he was met with polite scepticism. The breakthrough came, as Marianne Elliott has shown, when he approached Carnot in a public audience on 24 February, and it came for three reasons: his own persuasiveness, his exaggeration of the extent of revolutionary activity in Ireland, and his promise that an Irish rising would cripple the British war effort.[5] The latter in particular was music to Carnot's anglophobic ears, for Tone assured him that the arrival of 20,000 French troops in Ireland would bring a hundred thousand Irish to their support within weeks, and cripple British naval strength through the desertion of Irish sailors.

Carnot quickly took the project under his wing, hoping to make Ireland into England's Vendée, and on 19 June 1796 (1 messidor Year IV in the revolutionary calendar) the Directory formally made the decision to invade. The initial plan provided for a complicated three pronged attack, grafting the Irish expedition onto the previous project of a guerrilla invasion of England and integrating it with a naval expedition to India as well. 5,000 troops were to be landed in Galway Bay in mid-August to conquer Connaught, and the ships that carried them would then sail on to India to attack British possessions there. 5,000 more troops would meanwhile be landed on the Yorkshire coast in England, and 6,000 men – including a cavalry detachment – sent to Galway to reinforce the initial landing. Among them was to be a free corps (*Légion des Francs*) of criminals and former *chouans* (guerrilla fighters) from Brittany and the Vendée. A group of 5,000 foreign deserters was also to be brought over from Holland, bringing the total invasion force to around 16,000.[6] Hoche was not initially designated as commander of the invasion force because the Directory considered it to too small for a general of his stature, but four days later Carnot reversed that decision, asking him to command it 'if your absence (from Brittany) would not lead to fresh disturbances and if someone in your army could act as your temporary replacement'.[7] Hoche welcomed the challenge and was officially appointed commander on 20 July 1796 (2 thermidor IV), with orders to assemble a force of 15,000 troops and officers from his army in the west. He was an able and ambitious general who had risen rapidly through the ranks of the army since 1789. An adjutant-general in 1793 on the north-eastern front, he had gone on to command the Army of the Moselle in Alsace before becoming commander of the Army of the Coasts of Brest in 1794, then later the Army of the Ocean, where he had brought the civil war in Brittany and the Vendée to an end, defeating an émigré landing organised by the British at Quiberon Bay in July 1795. Still only 28 years old, he was intelligent and decisive. His experience against the peasant rebels in the

13

west of France equipped him with military and negotiating experience that would have been invaluable in Ireland, and he quickly struck up a friendship with Tone which, across the language barrier, was based on mutual trust and affection.[8]

By late July Hoche had modified the original invasion plan to a two stage operation, doubling the troop numbers involved: 15,000 troops were now to sail from Brest in the first wave of the invasion, with a second wave of 16,000 following within weeks. However the timing had already begun to slip, for an August sailing was now out of the question, since Hoche only arrived in Brest in late September because of negotiating delays in Rennes. When he arrived he was quickly appalled by the slow pace of the naval preparations. The Naval Minister, Laurent Truguet, was fully behind the expedition, but the vice-admiral in command of the fleet in Brest, Villaret-Joyeuse, was distinctly hostile. His heart was set on the expedition to India that had been built into the initial plans, and not on the detour to Ireland which he regarded as both unnecessary and dangerous because of British naval superiority. The Directory only ruled out the Indian expedition altogether on 13 October, but by then Villaret-Joyeuse's attitude had already alienated Hoche to such an extent that the Directory replaced him on 5 November with Morard de Galles, an experienced sailor in his mid-50s. Yet Villaret-Joyeuse had not been the only problem, for the French navy itself was in poor condition. An impressive boat-building programme in the 1770s and 1780s had equipped it with a number of modern ships, bringing its size to close to that of the British navy, but the revolution had led to mass emigration among its officers, most of whom were from noble families, and to increased discipline problems among sailors. Seven out of nine admirals had resigned, only three out of eighteen rear-admirals remained in their posts, and three quarters of the ships' captains had gone. Several ships had already been lost to British naval action in the Mediterranean and the Atlantic, while soaring inflation and crippling money shortages meant that sailors and dock workers wages were seriously in arrears. The preparation work therefore went slowly, the weeks dragged by, the troops grew restless and Hoche became exasperated. On 8 December he wrote to the Directory threatening to resign from the project altogether, and five days later the Directory cancelled the expedition, in response to an urgent call from Bonaparte for troop reinforcements in Italy. But by the time their letter had reached Brest it was too late: the preparations had been completed, the ships were ready, and the fleet set sail on 15 December.

It left in some disarray.[9] During the three mile passage from the inner harbour through the narrow straits of the Goulet de Brest, four boats collided with each other, causing minor damage. It was an ominous omen and worse was to follow, for Morard's original plan had been to avoid detection by a British naval squadron patrolling off Brest (or to decoy them into thinking that his destination was Portugal) by reaching the open sea through the southerly route of the Raz de Seine. However, during the afternoon of 16 December he changed his mind at the last moment, opting for the westerly Iroise Channel instead. By then most of the fleet was heading for the Raz, and although Morard used cannon fire to alert them to the change of direction, the noise was confused with distress signals fired by one of the fleet, the *Séduisant*, which had hit rocks and was sinking. As a result many vessels knew nothing about the change of plan and the fleet split, with 17 ships going through the Raz (including the *Indomptable* which carried Wolfe Tone), and the rest (including the *Fraternité* which carried Morard de Galles and Hoche) through the Iroise. Most of the fleet linked up again on 19 December off Mizen Head, but the *Fraternité* did not, for it had been blown further to the south-west after leaving the French coast and was to make no further contact with the main body of the fleet for the remainder of the expedition. Tone dryly commented in his journal: 'I believe it was the first instance of an admiral in a clean frigate, with moderate weather and moonlight nights, parting company with the fleet'.

With Hoche and Morard effectively out of the operation, their second in commands, Emmanuel de Grouchy and François Joseph Bouvet, took over. Grouchy was a former noble, just thirty years old, who had remained in the army after 1789 and served under Hoche in the Vendée. Bouvet was thirteen years his senior and had extensive naval experience in the Far East and the Atlantic. Once off Mizen Head, they opened letters written by Hoche and Morard before the departure, which contained the detailed orders for the landing. It was then that they discovered that their destination was Bantry Bay, information which had been kept secret until then to avoid news leaking out to British spies active in Brest. Tone's preference had been for a landing in Leinster or Ulster, where the United Irishmen and Defenders were thickest on the ground, but the Directory was worried by British naval cover in those areas and had plumped for Galway Bay instead in its plan of 19 June. By September news of this had leaked to the British, and Carnot therefore left the final choice to Hoche and Morard. They opted in mid-November for Bantry, as it had been the scene of a previous successful French landing in 1689, the south-west coast offered a good chance of the fleet avoiding British naval cover, Bantry had an excellent natural harbour, and it was just 270 miles (or 36 hours sailing time) from Brest. Carnot also considered Cork a crucial town to capture quickly after landing because it provided most of the victualling stores for the British navy.

According to Morard's plan, the fleet was to sail to Mizen Head, then pass Three Castle Head and Sheep's Head, before turning into Bantry Bay. There it would choose between three alternative mooring places, depending on the prevailing winds, and disembark the infantry as soon as possible. By the morning of 21 December the fleet, reduced by now to 35 ships, had slightly overshot its mark and found itself heading for Dursey Island. However, it was fortunate enough to pick up Irish pilots, who had come out to meet it in the mistaken belief that it was an English squadron returning from Jamaica, and who then agreed to help it enter the bay. That proved difficult, because it meant battling head-on into strong south-easterly winds, and by the late afternoon of 22 December only fifteen ships, carrying some 6,400 men, had made it in. Among them was the *Immortalité* carrying Bouvet and Grouchy, but Bouvet compounded his difficulties by anchoring due east of Bear

Island, in mid-channel, rather than in the strait between the island and the mainland, as stipulated in Morard's plans. That position would have given the ships shelter from the wind and the failure to reach it proved crucial, for on the following day all fifteen ships were buffeted by gales and driving snow until the late afternoon. On the morning of 24 December the winds dropped and, after a brief meeting with his officers, Grouchy requested Bouvet to prepare for an immediate landing. Bouvet ordered his ships to proceed to the anchorage at Bearhaven, but after several hours of tacking they had made little progress and a strong gale then sprang up around 6p.m. which halted progress altogether. It developed into a storm for the next two days, ruling out all hopes of a landing, and on the evening of Christmas Day the *Immortalité* dragged its anchors and found itself being blown towards Bear Island. Bouvet promptly decided to leave the bay, using megaphone and cannon fire to order the other ships to follow, and was blown almost three hundred miles back out into the Atlantic. However only one of the other ships, the *Platon*, realised that he was leaving and the rest stayed on until the following day. The senior remaining naval officer, Bedout, then called a brief meeting at which it was agreed to weigh anchor and head for the mouth of the Shannon in the hope of meeting up with the rest of the fleet, which had remained outside the bay. Nine ships reached there by the morning of 28 December, but after waiting twenty-four hours for the remainder of the fleet to show up, they abandoned hope and headed back to France, arriving in Brest on New Year's Day. The *Droits de l'Homme*, which became separated from the others on the way out of Bantry, never made it back at all. Spotted by two British frigates as she approached the Brittany coast, she ran aground on a sand bank in Audierne Bay and, of the 1,350 men on board, almost a thousand were drowned

Bedout's decision meant that there was no French presence in Bantry Bay on 28 December, but on the following day the ships that had failed to make it in with Bouvet on 21–22 December, now began to struggle in, anchoring off the north side of Whiddy Island. One of them, the frigate *Surveillante*, arrived in on 31 December but was leaking so badly that she had to be abandoned and scuttled a mile off shore, on the Glengarriff side of the bay, two days later. The senior naval officer in this second wave, Commodore Durand-Linois, now found himself with 4 ships of the line, 4 frigates and some 4,000 troops at his disposal. But it was a small force, its supplies were running low, it lacked any artillery, and both Durand-Linois and his fellow officers were convinced – mistakenly as it turned out – that a militia force of at least 5,000 was ready to confront them if they landed. So on 2 January it was decided to leave the bay and cruise outside for two days in the hope of meeting up with the rest of the fleet there. The departure was delayed for two days – ironically enough because of a period of flat calm – but they finally left on the night of 5–6 January and cruised for three days south-west of Dursey Island before returning to Brest by 13 January.

The only remaining major actors in the drama were Hoche and Morard de Galles, on board the *Fraternité*. After the fiasco leaving Brest, they had been blown out to the south-west by the gales and made matters worse by taking evasive action to avoid what they mistakenly believed to be British ships. By 28 December they were 200 miles south-west of the Irish coast but the wind then switched back to the west, enabling them to make their way back towards Bantry. By 30 December they were some 28 miles south west of Dursey, but by now had met up with the *Révolution* which been in the bay with Bouvet on 21 December but lost its bowsprit, cables and anchor in a collision during the storm on 26 December. It was carrying 2,200 men reduced to half rations, in a perilously unseaworthy condition, so Morard and Hoche decided on the afternoon of 31 December that all hopes of a successful landing had gone, and that they would accompany the *Révolution* back to Brest. In fact, had they continued on into Bantry they would have found Durand-Linois there with his four ships and 4,000 men, trapped by calm conditions. But it is unlikely that Hoche would have taken the risk of a landing with such depleted forces, and the decision to return to Brest probably made little difference to the expedition's outcome.

Of the 45 ships that had set sail on 15 December, only 35 returned to Brest and many of them were so badly damaged that they needed several months of refitting work before they could take to sea again. Apart from the loss of the *Séduisante* on the exit from Brest and the scuttling of the *Surveillante* in Bantry, the *Scévola* had sunk on 30 December (although all 820 men on board had been saved), the *Droits de l'Homme* had sunk in Audierne Bay and the *Tortue*, the *Atalante*, the *Ville de Lorient*, the *Suffren* and the *Allègre*, had all been captured. Over 1,500 soldiers and sailors had been drowned and a further 2,000 had been captured by the British. Those that survived were shattered by the experience, and when rumours of a second attempt began to circulate in Brest in mid-January, there was a threat of a mutiny. The whole affair had been a disaster, plagued by adverse weather, hampered by incompetent seamanship and crippled by a sizeable slice of sheer bad luck. The weather conditions obviously played a central role, for the gales that hit the fleet as it approached Bantry and continued intermittently over the next two weeks, made a landing difficult. Gales are hardly unexpected off the south-west of Ireland during the winter months, and the precise weather conditions prevailing at the time are analysed in detail elsewhere in this book by Dr John Tyrrell, yet the difficulties that they caused were not insuperable. Instead they were exacerbated by a series of naval errors. The first of these was Morard's decision to change his exit route from Brest at the last moment on 16 December, for this split the fleet and removed himself and Hoche from the main body of the expedition altogether. This was crucial to the fate of the expedition, for Hoche alone had the charisma and ability to overcome the difficulties encountered in Bantry and would certainly have acted more quickly and decisively than Grouchy did when the wind dropped on 24 December. He might even have attempted to land the infantry on the south side of the bay (instead of at Bear Haven), at Gortnakilly or on one of the beaches nearby which were sheltered from the prevailing easterly wind. There would have been risks involved in both options, but both he and his troops had considerable experience of operating in adverse conditions in Brittany, and a landing then would have opened the route to Bantry and Cork. Grouchy was a worthy general but, despite his later attempts to blame Hoche's lack of detailed instructions for the failure of the expedition, he lacked the energy and ability that Hoche possessed.

In addition to Hoche's absence, the inexperience of many of the sailors, and the poor quality of much of their equipment, were also important. Poor seamanship caused the collisions that happened leaving Brest, it recurred in navigational problems that the fleet had in approaching Bantry, and surfaced again in the difficulty they experienced in entering the bay. Bouvet's ships struggled in against the wind on 21 and 22 December, but a larger number under the command of admirals Richéry and Nielly stayed outside, unable to make it in. Bouvet then anchored on 23 December off the east shore of Bear Island, in mid-channel, leaving his ships exposed to the easterly gales, when Morard's orders clearly indicated that he was to pass between the eastern end of the island and Roancarrig to the Bear Haven anchorage, or tack his way up the length of the bay to anchor off Whiddy. Either would have provided welcome shelter from the storm, and left him well placed for the landing operation, but Bouvet did neither. A third factor on the naval side was fear, for throughout the expedition naval officers were convinced that they risked a full scale engagement with the British navy: that had been one of Villaret-Joyeuse's reasons for opposing the expedition in the first place, it had caused the fiasco leaving Brest on 16 December, and the fear of entrapment haunted French sailors once they were in Bantry from 22 December onwards. It was the main reason why Bouvet left the bay so quickly on 26 December and the reason why the second wave of ships left on 5 January. The irony, however, was that between 22 December and 6 January not a single British soldier or ship appeared in the Bantry area. The French had the seas around the southwest of Ireland largely to themselves and, had they known their good fortune, they might well have stayed longer and landed the troops.

If they had landed, Hoche's instructions on what to do in

– and with – Ireland were clearly laid out in correspondence between Hoche and the Directory over the summer of 1796.[10] In their letter to him of 19 June the Directors explained their decision to invade Ireland on grounds which had been largely defined by Tone over the preceding months, namely that Ireland was suffering under the 'odious yoke' of England, and that a considerable force of 'defenders' was ready to rise as soon as the French arrived. To those they added a third reason, the blow the invasion would deal to England. In Carnot's words: 'To detach Ireland from England, is to reduce England to a second rate power, and take from it much of its maritime superiority. There is little point in elaborating on the advantages to France that Irish independence would bring'. Victory in Ireland would bring about 'the fall of the most irreconcilable and most dangerous of our enemies. I see in it tranquillity for France for centuries to come and ... a new career of glory for yourself'. If Ireland was to serve as a stepping stone towards the defeat of England – and this was certainly Hoche's own priority – it was also to be transformed in the process, for the Directors gave at least lip service to Tone's assertion that the vast majority of Irish people wanted to live under a French style republic.[11] Hoche was therefore advised that 'the closer the Irish get to the system of government that we have adopted, the more *we* can rely on a permanent alliance between France and their country'. To ensure that this happened he was urged to take the political initiative as soon as he landed and to prevent Irish radicals imposing their own agenda. Instead he was to take command of any Irish army that materialised, control government until a peace settlement had been concluded with England, and supervise all government officials. Above all he was to control political life himself and avoid being sidelined as the mere commander of an auxiliary force in an Irish insurrection. The Directors were convinced that this would cause no problems, 'for you will always direct the new governing agents according to the wishes of the Directory, towards liberty and towards the happiness which ensures it'. They also urged him to use persuasion rather than force wherever possible, and to conduct Irish affairs with 'such tact that they never realise the hand which is conducting them towards independence and the happiness of their country'.

The broad framework within which Hoche was to use that 'tact' was also laid out by the Directory, as he was advised to allow the Catholic Committee and United Irishmen to form a consultative assembly soon after his arrival, until elections could be held for a more permanent assembly. This assembly was to be kept small, with two or three representatives per county, and he could dissolve it if a majority emerged that was favourable to retaining the link with Britain. There were therefore limits to the democracy that he was to export to Ireland, for the aim of the assembly was to produce an Irish republic on the French model, with a written constitution and bicameral legislature. If the Irish insisted on a monarchy instead, they could have one as long as the monarch was pro-French, a well-known opponent of England and a Catholic – a proviso regarded as a cast-iron way of ensuring that the two countries would remain at loggerheads. This particular proviso may have been the work of Carnot's adviser in the War Ministry, General Clarke, a second-generation Irishman who doubted Tone's claims of widespread republicanism in Ireland and was convinced that a Jacobite restoration was more probable than a republic. As for religion, the Directory's clear hope was to encourage the growth of a secular ideology, similar to that prevailing in France since dechristianisation and the separation of Church and State had destroyed the wealth and power of the Catholic Church. Yet it was well aware that the Irish might not yet be ready for that kind of change, and conceded that the three major denominations – Anglican, Presbyterian and Catholic – would probably have to stay in existence for the foreseeable future. Nevertheless Anglicanism would be disestablished, as all Churches would have to pay for their own priests, and Catholicism was to be kept under control 'as its doctrines are opposed to the healthy institutions of philosophy and morality and to the progress of knowledge'. If the collapse of British rule nevertheless encouraged Catholics 'to free themselves from the superstition of the Church of Rome, to which three-quarters of the population are currently submitted' –

something which the Directory clearly hoped for – they were not to be allowed to drift towards Anglicanism or Presbyterianism, but encouraged to adopt 'natural' religion and become deists. Finally, there was an economic price to paid for liberation and enlightenment, for Ireland was expected to pay for the costs of the French expedition in the form of cash payments and future trade advantages.[12]

Quite how this would have all worked out is impossible to say. The Directors clearly based their plan on the information given to them by Tone, who exaggerated the strength of republican support in Ireland, while taking into account the possibility that things might not turn out exactly the way he predicted. It has to be said that in Belgium and the German Rhineland the behaviour of French soldiers, their anti-clericalism and their economic demands for food, horses and other supplies, quickly alienated the local population. French troops would have needed supplies soon after landing, and they certainly needed horses. How easy this would have been to obtain in the south-west is not clear, but it is clear that the potential for civilian-military conflict was there. On the other hand, Hoche was an astute general who knew how to handle civilian-military relations. The orders that his troops received before departure stressed the need for discipline, and it seems reasonable to assume that a reasonable degree of co-operation could have enabled the whole thing to go off easily.

Yet we shall never know. All we do know is that Hoche was transferred to the army of the Sambre-et-Meuse in the Rhineland immediately after his return. Tone went with him and, for a short time in the spring of 1797 after Bonaparte signed a preliminary truce with the Austrians at Leoben in April, there were hopes that Hoche would organise a second invasion. Yet by then France was negotiating with England and policy makers had decided that Ireland would first have to mount its own revolt before it could expect French help. Hoche's premature death in September finally ended all hopes of action in 1797 and the only sequel that year came in the form of the ill-fated Fishguard expedition. Four ships left Brest on 16 February with a small force of ex-prisoners, soldiers renowned for their indiscipline, and a handful of troops that had been to Bantry and back, all commanded by a seventy year old American merchant, William Tate. Their destination was Bristol, where they were meant to land and cause havoc on the lines outlined in Carnot's plan of the previous spring, but instead they landed close to Fishguard, in Pembrokeshire, on the night of 22–23 February. Half starved and wholly undisciplined, they raided a nearby farmhouse which, quite by chance, contained several crates of wine retrieved from a shipwreck on the coast several days before. That ruined any hope of even transient success, for they quickly drank the lot and then went on a drunken rampage, raiding local farms for food before being rounded up by the local militia. The whole sorry episode lasted little more than 48 hours. Two Welshmen were killed and a woman shot in the leg; four French soldiers died, two shot by a farmer for cattle stealing, another pitchforked to death by a cottager for stealing food and beer, and a fourth shot by the militia. Among the survivors was a young Irishman, Barry St Ledger, who claimed that he had attempted to maintain discipline by warning his men that looters would be shot, only to receive the reply that they could shoot as well as he could.[13] It was a pitiful end to a poor winter for the French, and a disappointing winter for Tone, the Defenders and the United Irishmen.

THE WEATHER AND POLITICAL DESTINY

JOHN TYRRELL

One of the primary reasons given for the failure of the French invasion at Bantry Bay in 1796 was the severe weather.[1] The failure of the French expedition may be one of the few historical events of significance to Ireland in which the weather played a decisive role. This chapter presents the results of historical research to reconstruct the daily weather conditions which prevailed in December 1796 and the nature of the storms and other weather conditions which overcame the French fleet. It also explores the reasonable expectations that there may have been of the weather in December 1796 as a basis for assessing its role in the outcome of the events that took place.

THE HISTORICAL RECONSTRUCTION OF THE WEATHER

There are a number of data sources available for this task. Since the conditions at sea are critical some of the most valuable data are contained in the logbooks of ships. Each vessel of the English navy was required to keep two logbooks, the Master's log and the Captain's log. The Master's logbook recorded the hour, the ship's speed and course, wind conditions and 'other remarks'. The latter recorded a range of other weather conditions. When under sail this record was an hourly one, yielding an immense amount of data. The record was briefer when in harbour, being made 'only' four times a day. The Captain often copied what was already in the Master's log, so that source generally yields little new information. However, with the deployment of a very large number of ships of the line, frigates and sloops patrolling the Channel and the seas around Ireland, escorting convoys of merchantmen, stationed in Irish and other ports, the logbook entries can be validated by thorough cross-checking. (This method has been used successfully to reconstruct Irish weather during the 1750s).[2] Supplementing this is Wolfe Tone's own record of the weather contained in his daily diary, in which he made copious comments on the weather.[3]

The eighteenth century saw the beginnings of instrumental weather measurement and observations and some of these data are available for the present study. Armagh Observatory commenced observations in 1795, and in December 1796 has air temperatures and barometric pressure readings three times each day, together with wind direction and records of visual observations.[4] Elsewhere in Ireland, Richard Kirwan was recording pressure, temperature, rainfall and wind (1787–1808) in Dublin, but only monthly summaries have been published.[5] In England, Thomas Barker of Rutland was using meteorological instruments to record the weather between 1748 and 1798, but for 1796 only his monthly summaries, as communicated to the Royal Society, have been published[6] as is also the case for data recorded at Edinburgh.[7]

Observations of wind direction and speed were used to construct the broad pattern of atmospheric pressure between longitudes 5 degrees E and 25 degrees W, and latitudes 35 degrees N and 60 degrees N for each day between 1 December 1796 and 5 January 1797, based on the midday observations. On to these synoptic charts were added other observed weather conditions. In this way, the extent and sequence of the weather affecting the operation of the French and English fleets was established. These maps show that December 1796 can be divided into four periods as far as the impact of weather upon French operations was concerned. These were:

1–16 December: for the preparation, planning and eventual departure of the French fleet from Brest.
17–20 December: when the fleet was dispersed and progressed very slowly into Irish coastal waters.
21–27 December: during which the fleet attempted to land at Bantry Bay.
27 December–2 January 1797: when the new rendezvous also failed.

1–16 DECEMBER

The first half of the month was dominated by easterly winds. These were produced by high pressure to the north and north-east of Britain and Ireland and an area of low pressure west of the Bay of Biscay (Fig. 1). At Armagh the atmospheric pressure was above 30 inches of mercury (1016 hPa) from 8–16 December and even during the first week of the month there were only three days when the pressure was significantly lower. This resulted in the area of high pressure extending considerably further south of its modern mean position for December,[8] and produced persistent easterly winds for the first half of the month. If the French fleet had been assured of their naval superiority over the English these pressure and wind conditions would have been very favourable for launching the expedition and reaching Ireland. However, this was not the case. If opposed, the French had few doubts that they would lose out in a direct encounter with the English. It has been argued that French naval policy had left a legacy of neglect as far as the fleet was concerned, which ensured that the French navy was second-rate. This meant that a successful landing in Ireland required that the expedition avoid the English fleet.[9]

At the time that Wolfe Tone joined the fleet at Brest and boarded the *Indomptable,* he was informed that twenty-six English ships of the line and frigates had been waiting just off Ushant (the modern Isle d'Ouessant) for up to ten weeks. Behind this line of defence Admiral Kingsmill at Cork deployed *HMS Kangaroo, HMS Hazard* and *HMS Diana* to patrol between Lundy and Cape Clear and along the west coast of Ireland.[10] Kingsmill's concern was not just the security of the Irish coast from a potential invasion, but keeping secure the trade routes from the West Indies to Cork and from Cork to Lisbon. Even during times of heightened tension privateers plundered the trade routes. One such, *La Musette,* was captured and brought to Cork Harbour by *HMS Hazard* during the period of these events.[11]

Tone had a strategy to counter the blockade which de-

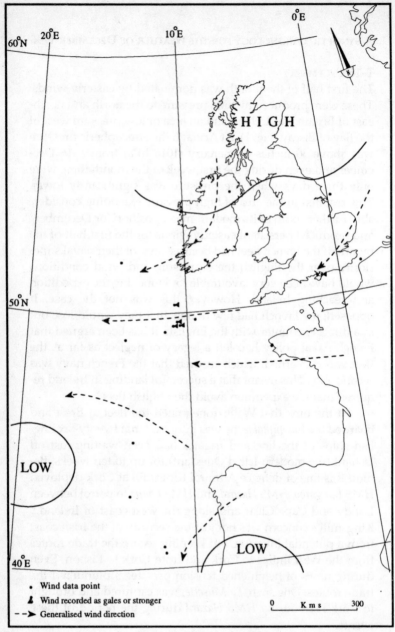

Figure 1 – 15 December 1796

pended upon the weather conditions. This required a north-east gale to displace the English fleet westwards and allow the three or four fastest French ships to leave Brest under cover of darkness with about 2,000 troops. This group would sail rapidly to the north of Ireland to support an imminent rising there. He then expected the English fleet to withdraw and redeploy to deal with the threat in the north. This would open up the way for the main embarkation landing in the south, putting the English land forces between two fires which, Tone thought, would be decisive (Fig. 2). For a variety of reasons this strategy was turned down.

The only alternative which Tone thought might stand some chance of success, also depended upon suitable weather conditions. Westerly winds would merely trap the expedition in Brest harbour, make the troops ill and continue to use up the supplies of food. But a westerly storm of two or three days duration would be different. This would displace the English fleet eastwards up the Channel opening up the sea for the entire French fleet before the English could return to their blockading positions. While Tone preferred the north-easterly plan, once it was turned down he saw the westerly plan to offer the only viable alternative. Most of the options, therefore, depended on the weather.

16–20 DECEMBER
The waiting ended on 16 December. But there was no change in the weather at this stage. The wind was still easterly, providing some help for the journey, otherwise it would appear to be the prevailing view among the French that weather could be left to chance. However, the fleet had been reinforced a few days earlier and was now at its maximum strength. Waiting around had already begun to deplete their stores, so it was clear that further delay would achieve little. Vice-Admiral Morard de Galles gave the order to leave the harbour by a southerly passage through the narrow and dangerous Raz de Seine, instead of through the main Iroise Channel. Although the latter led directly to the Atlantic it was also much closer to the English blockading fleet positioned north of Ushant. To

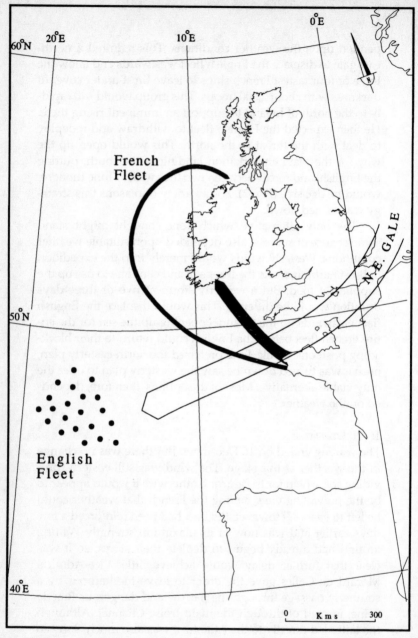

French
Fleet

N.E. GALE

English
Fleet

0°E
10°E
20°E
60°N
50°N
40°E

0   Kms   300

Figure 2 – Wolfe Tone's Plan

further conceal the manoeuvre from the English it was carried out at night. The effect was to split up the French fleet.

The *Indomptable*, with Wolfe Tone and Captain Bedout on board, was one of twelve vessels which successfully passed the Raz (although with great difficulty). Also among these was the *Immortalité* on which were Rear-Admiral Bouvet and General Grouchy. Tone records that this group increased to 18 during the following day.

On the flagship *Fraternité* were Vice-Admiral Morard de Galles and all the other leaders of the expedition. At the last moment De Galles considered the risks of the Raz passage to be too great because his pilot advised that a small change in the wind direction from easterly to east-south-east would require the vessels to tack.[12] Therefore, he signalled the fleet to leave through the main channel. Amid great confusion some of the fleet were able to follow but they were chased by the English. The *Fraternité* sustained damage and sailed far into the Atlantic to escape.

Most of the fleet was now with Tone, Bedout, Bouvet and Grouchy and for these 17 December was a good day. The weather was benign and enabled some of those who had been scattered to find one another as they took a course to the west-north-west with a favourable wind behind them.

At this point the weather began to change. Wind records show that a weak frontal depression was slowly advancing from the south-west and was about to replace the easterlies which had persisted for so long. The Armagh pressure data indicate a weakening of the high pressure area which had dominated the weather for so long. The depression brought with it moist tropical air from the direction of the Azores. As this gradually cooled during its progress north-eastwards between latitudes 40 and 50 degrees an extensive bank of thick fog and mist was produced. This enveloped both the French and the English fleets during the night of the seventeenth and throughout the eighteenth (Fig. 3). At times this was so thick that it was not possible to see a ship's length. While this gave a cloak of invisibility to the French, it also hindered those still scattered from finding one another. In addition to this, the

31

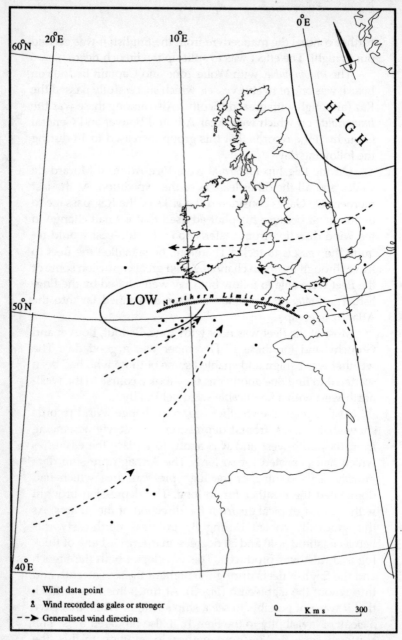

- • Wind data point
- ☊ Wind recorded as gales or stronger
- – – > Generalised wind direction

0   K m s   300

Figure 3 – 18 December 1796

32

wind was very slack so progress towards Ireland was slow.

There were important contrasts in these conditions over relatively short distances. Latitude 50 N appears to have been a significant boundary. The fog persisted over the Atlantic approaches to Ireland south of this latitude where the majority of the English fleet were deployed. But to the north of this and all along the Irish coast the weather was clear. Here, much further ahead of the slow-moving warm front the winds were still strong easterlies. The only English ships in that area of sea were *HMS Magnanime* in Cork harbour, *HMS Diana* patrolling off Berehaven and *HMS Kangaroo* off Ventry. The bulk of the English fleet positioned to intercept any French move were groping around in the fog – which was much more to their disadvantage than to the French.

The French did not realise the advantage the fog had given them. They passed through it (though some haze persisted) and emerged with most of the English fleet behind them and effectively immobilised. The wind was also much in their favour, being easterly and not very strong. This undoubtedly aided a number of ships joining up again with the main group as they emerged from the fog one by one, so that most of the fleet had come together again by the end of 20 December.

The low pressure moved only slowly over the next two days, with little change in the position of the fog. Its movement was eastwards, pushing across southern England and the North Sea. As this was happening, a following cold front travelling in its wake introduced cooler air and winds which veered to the north-west. So, on the afternoon of 19 December, as the French completed their journey towards Mizen Head, they found the wind picking up and becoming more of a head wind than a following wind. These conditions would have been favourable for entering Bantry Bay and were timed just right for their arrival. But since the *Fraternité*, with both the commander-in-chief and the admiral on board, was still missing, instructions prepared for this contingency were followed. These required them to wait for five days off the Mizen Head to see whether contact with them could be restored.

The cold front passed over the southern parts of Ireland and Britain quite quickly and on 21 December pressure was beginning to build up again over Ireland and Britain. This reintroduced easterly winds along the southern coasts, while across northern Ireland and northern England the wind was still westerly (as shown by the observations at Armagh and Edinburgh). At first, the winds were light and sometimes quite variable, because of the slack pressure gradients.

The French expedition was still waiting. It was now within three leagues (16 km) of the coast. The cold polar air was typically clear and Wolfe Tone noted in his diary that he could see patches of snow on the mountains. The clarity of the air had also made it possible for the fleet to be seen from the land. Tone had been anxious about an early discovery which would give the defending forces on land plenty of time to prepare for them. Early on the morning of the 21 December the fleet was spotted by Mr White of Seafield House (now Bantry House). He passed on the information to Admiral Kingsmill at Cork.

Most of that snow observed by Tone would have been fresh from the frontal systems that had passed through. It was likely that the snow had been widespread across Ireland, since snow had also been recorded at Armagh. Whether this would have been a significant hindrance to the military in making a rapid response to a landing is difficult to tell. More snow was yet to come, so undoubtedly there would be some areas on land where it would pose mobility and other problems. But there was no immediate prospect of the French making a landing. The fleet had to wait around off the mouth of Bantry Bay, sometimes going with the wind and sometimes against it.

Another advancing low pressure system from the southwest brought much stronger winds than before. This was the first of three depressions that occurred after 21 December which were critical to the final sequence of events. This first one had its progress northwards blocked by relatively high pressure, deflecting it eastwards along a much more southerly track than winter storms tend to travel today. The northern part of a depression had easterly winds and it was these that now began to threaten the French. As the weather began to change on 22 December, Bouvet and Grouchy, now the leaders of the expedition, decided to wait no longer and to proceed up Bantry Bay to effect a landing. However, the easterlies quickly reached gale force. The gale became so severe that it became unexpectedly difficult to progress up the bay. Tone recorded:

> We have been tacking ever since eight this morning, and I am sure we have not gained one hundred yards; the wind is right ahead and the fleet dispersed ... At half-past six, cast anchor off Bere Island, being still four leagues from our landing place.

Strong gales continued through the night of 22–23 December and more snow fell on the mountains. The snow must have settled at a low altitude since Tone expected that the French would have to bivouac in it. But the greater effect was the further dispersal of the French fleet. Sixteen vessels, including Bouvet and Grouchy's *Immortalité*, were with Tone riding the storm at anchor, while another twenty had been blown back out to sea. The storm conditions prevented the usual strategy of placing a frigate at the entrance of the bay to give warning of the approach of any English vessels.

By 23 December there was still uncertainty in Cork as to the identification of the fleet off Bantry Bay. The report of Mr White was met with some scepticism in Cork. Kingsmill sent the report on to the Admiralty in London, but in his covering letter he commented:

> I do not credit their contents – I rather suspect it is the Lisbon or Quebec convoy – however, to ascertain the truth I instantly sent Lieutenant Pulling in the *Foxcutter* to Mizen Head – and expect he will be back in the morning.[13]

At first sight Kingsmill's view may seem surprising. But there had been a whole series of reported sightings of a French invasion fleet throughout December, all of which came to nothing. On 8 December, a major alarm had been raised by the sighting of a group of vessels which had not responded to signals. They were then lost in haze. Such false alarms could be expected because convoys of merchantmen regularly passed by offshore and visibility was often poor. Indeed, just at this time Kingsmill was expecting a large and valuable fleet of East India Company ships, due to arrive from St Helena, for which he was required to provide protection.[14]

It should not be overlooked that the storm conditions were causing some distress for the English fleet as well. In so far as this prevented the English fleet from locating the French, the French were fortunate. South of the Irish coast *HMS Kangaroo* was battling in hard easterly gales. It had sailed south from Ventry on 22 December and spotted the French fleet at the mouth of Bantry Bay. It struggled to Crookhaven to land dispatches there on 23 December for a hasty onward journey to Cork. Further out from the south coast *HMS Polyphemus* was struggling towards Cork with a split topsail, while the *HMS Diana* was half way between Crookhaven and the Old Head of Kinsale, trying to reach the shelter of Cork. The force of the storm was greatest over the sea south of Ireland. Further east in the English Channel no gales were reported on 22 or 23 December. But much more snow fell further east in the English Channel. Here the winds, though still easterly, were much lighter.

The intensity of what proved to be a series of easterly storms was yet to peak. In Bantry Bay on the morning of 24 December a council of war was held on the *Immortalité*. While it had been possible to row between ships to hold this meeting, the easterly headwind was still sufficiently strong to prevent any significant progress up the Bay. Tone recorded:

> This infernal easterly wind continues without remorse, and though we have been under way three or four hours, and made I believe three hundred tacks, we do not seem to my eyes to have gained one hundred yards in a straight line. One hour and a half of good wind would carry us up, and perhaps we may be yet two days.

This frustration was to last the whole day and is evident in Tone's wit:

At six cast anchor, having gained I think not less than fifty yards, to speak within bounds. The rapidity of our progress is the more amazing, when it is considered that we have been not much more than eight hours in covering that space of ground, and besides we have a cool refreshing breeze from the east, which is truly delightful.

Lieutenant Pulling had arrived in Bantry at 3pm on 24 December where he observed what he could of the fleet until darkness fell. The dense haze produced by the weather made a positive identification of the vessels in the bay very difficult. Poor visibility was to be a factor hindering both sides as the events unfolded. The French fleet underestimated the uncertainties this caused on land. From a distance of eight leagues (44 kms) Pulling could see through his spy-glass no flags nor pendants and could only conclude of the three most visible ships that 'I am certain were not English built'. He did not exclude the possibility that the fleet was an enemy, but he was confident that the weather would not allow them to sail higher up the bay than they were at that time.[15] Clearly, at this point the fleet was still a long way down the bay, still being seaward of Berehaven, confirming the slow progress reported by Tone.

The wind relented somewhat later that day as the depression that had caused the storms moved away. This lull was widespread, so that *HMS Polyphemus*, 17 leagues (94km) to the south-west of Dursey Island, recorded more moderate winds after fresh gales, *HMS Diana* off Crookhaven reported 'fresh breezes' (which allowed the pilot to come out of Crookhaven to pass on the news that the French were in Bantry Bay), the same wind conditions as reported by the *HMS Magnanime* and *HMS Penguin* in Cork Harbour. The change gave Tone hopes of being able to land the following day. There was no attempt to take immediate advantage of the relatively improved conditions, because of darkness.

But the respite was extremely brief. The second of the three significant depressions was now approaching Ireland rapidly from the south-west (Fig. 4). This also had strong gale force winds and followed a similar track as its predecessor, producing east and south-east gales over the same area. These

37

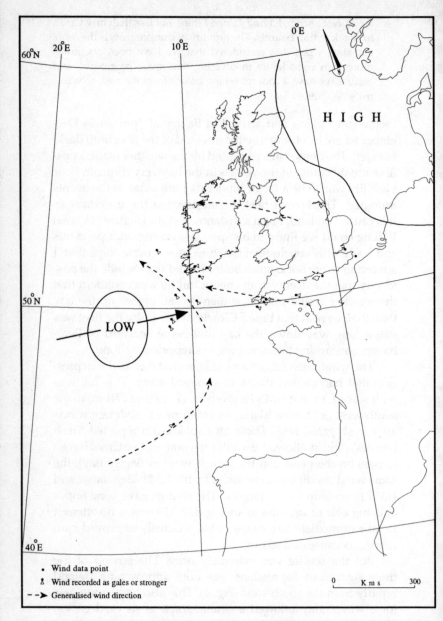

Figure 4 – 25 December 1796

winds burst on the scene in the early morning hours of 25 December, so that Tone wrote, 'it is absolutely impossible to work up to the landing place'. The gales persisted all day. The winds were probably stronger because they made impossible any communication by rowing boat. Tone recorded:

> We find it impossible to communicate with the General and the Admiral, who are in the *Immortalité*, nearly two leagues ahead, and the wind is now so high and foul, and the sea so rough, that no boat can live, so all communication is impracticable.

At nightfall on 25 December, the *Indomptable* put out two anchors to hold it in position in the face of the heavy gale. At 6.30pm it was surprised by the *Immortalité* appearing suddenly out of the darkness, hailing orders to cut its cable and put to sea and quickly disappearing into the darkness as it went before the wind. Because of the storm's severity and the darkness the *Indomptable* decided to wait for morning to confirm these unexpected orders. Again, the lack of communication because of the weather conditions prevented decisive action. Admiral Bouvet had decided to leave the bay for fear of losing the fleet to the storm. Some had already been blown out to sea or could barely hold their position in the bay, anchors were dragging, and critically, food was running very short.[16]

By 25 December, Admiral Kingsmill in Cork had changed his mind. Now he was convinced that he was dealing with a French invasion fleet. Reports were coming in which left him in no doubt. The news from *HMS Kangaroo* had reached him via Crookhaven, while further reports from Mr Bailey, a surgeon at Bearhaven, and Mr White, together with the observations from Lieutenant Pulling, all pointed to the same conclusion.[17] But Kingsmill appears to have been more concerned about the threat posed by the enemy and the weather to the safety of the convoys expected in Cork than the possibility of a landing by the French.[18]

For those still in the bay the morning of 26 December brought no improvement to the weather. Indeed, there was another problem. With the gales continuing, fog became an additional hazard, and Tone recorded that 'the fog is so thick that we cannot see a ship's length ahead'. This must have been a relatively local phenomenon. *HMS Polyphemus* off the west coast and *HMS Diana* off Crookhaven reported only haze. In Cork harbour there was neither fog nor haze. However, the fog in the bay was not long-lasting since later in the day those on the *Indomptable* were clearly aware of what was happening to other vessels in the bay. These had also remained to ride out the storm and were referred to by Tone as 'our little squadron'. Additional departures were the *Révolution*, which cut her cables to return to sea, followed during the night by the *Patriote*, *Pluton* and *Nicomede*, reducing the fighting force in the bay to eight by the morning of 27 December.

On the morning of 26 December Tone became convinced of the futility of proceeding any further. It was assumed that the Admiral and the General in the *Immortalité* had set course to return to France. The remaining ships were also conscious of the length of time that they had been confined to the bay without being able to land, thereby losing their early advantage over their enemy. Landing the force in Bantry Bay now appeared impracticable. But it was the weather that Tone held ultimately responsible for closing off his options, except to retreat. Tone recorded:

> Notwithstanding all our blunders, it is the dreadful stormy weather and the easterly winds, which have been blowing furiously and without intermission since we made Bantry Bay, that have ruined us.

On the morning of 27 December it was considered safe to take the remainder of the force back out of Bantry Bay. Tone was eager to adopt a new strategy rather than to abandon the expedition altogether. The remaining senior officers took advantage of the easing weather conditions to leave their ships for a council of war. There was unanimity to leave the bay and proceed to the Shannon where it was hoped they would be able to reassemble some of the scattered fleet and be able to make a successful landing. As the depression moved away, so the wind swung round to a southerly direction, which favoured the new strategy. The remaining fleet of 10 ships, including seven frigates, left the bay and faced the open sea.

27 DECEMBER–2 JANUARY

The weather was now to take a final hand in the affairs of the expedition. It was the weather encountered after leaving Bantry Bay, that was to destroy all hopes of making the alternative landing. Each of the storms that had been encountered had been fiercer than its predecessor. The third depression of the sequence since 21 December produced the fiercest storm of the month. This arrived on the night of 27–28 December and provoked the only comment by Tone which anticipated a change in the weather. Late in the day, as the *Indomptable* manoeuvred out of the bay, he observed that there was 'every appearance of a stormy night', and this hastened preparations to get out of the bay and away from the dangerous coastline.

The storm was more than had been expected. It was 'a perfect hurricane' with an exceptionally rough sea, which seriously damaged and almost sank the *Indomptable*. The storm caused widespread damage in the south-west. For example, in Cork city it was reported that three vessels broke their moorings and were dashed with violence against Patrick's Bridge.[19] But the wind abated and Tone's group of vessels reached their rendezvous off the Shannon estuary and began to wait for others to join them. Some had not been so fortunate. In particular, the *Impatient* was wrecked off Crookhaven. The few survivors that made it to shore thought the fleet had dispersed and reported discontent among the crew and a shortage of rations right from the start of the expedition.[20]

The depression that had produced this fearsome storm on the twenty-eighth had moved quickly northwards to reach northern Ireland on the twenty-ninth (Fig. 5). Although by this time the winds had abated off the south-west coast and had become west to south-west in direction, they were still strong and continued to be hazardous. Further depressions produced gale force winds and changes in wind direction between north-west (which would assist the return journey to France) and south-west as the depressions crossed over Ireland, until 1 January when the weather eased.

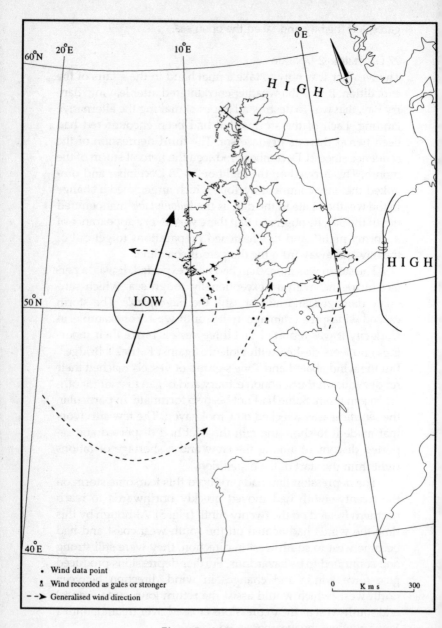

Figure 5 – 28 December 1796

But before these arrived, Wolfe Tone decided that enough was enough. At four in the morning on 29 December the decision was made to leave for France. All the delays induced by the severity of the weather now meant that supplies were so low that there was hardly sufficient to get everyone back to France. This did not prevent opportunistic diversions on the return journey. Off the coast of Ireland the *Indomptable* sank a merchant vessel travelling between Lisbon and Cork. But that was the last of the action Wolfe Tone was to experience. Other encounters were less hostile. One 74-gun ship with 2,000 men on board was encountered by the *Winchester Trumper* from Gibraltar 139 km to the south-west of Cape Clear. But the French vessel was pumping furiously and only wanted to know where it was. Other traders from the Lisbon and Quebec convoys, themselves dispersed by the weather, ran into remnants of the French fleet off Cape Clear and Mizen Head. But they escaped from the French due to the extremely poor weather which saved them from being boarded.[21]

While Tone headed back to France there were new arrivals in Bantry Bay. Late on 30 December five remnants of the original fleet arrived, which Kingsmill considered had not been there before and which had hopes of joining up with the rest of the fleet.[22] The following day others joined them and precautions were taken for the unlikely event that such a small force would attempt a landing from their anchorage off Whiddy Island. But they sailed at 3pm on 2 January, scuttling the *Surveillante*, the remaining nine vessels that had gathered taking advantage of a south-east gale, although they did not completely clear the bay until 4 January.[23] The *Fraternité*, with Morard de Galles, Hoche and Briux on board, did not reach the bay at all. Having avoided the English by sailing far to the westward, it headed back towards Bantry Bay and met the badly damaged *Révolution* taking men off the sinking *Scévola* and learned the fate of the expedition. Continuing south-east gales with very poor visibility delayed their pursuit by the squadron from Cork, which was not able to leave Cork until 4 January.[24]

There were also late arrivals at the Shannon rendezvous,

where two of the fleet had arrived on 1 January. But rightly concluding that any others who had weathered the storm of 29 December had abandoned further attempts at a landing, they departed on 2 January.[25]

HOW EXCEPTIONAL WAS THE WEATHER OF DECEMBER 1796?

If the storms of 1796 were exceptional and outside what might reasonably be expected of the climate it is possible to understand the apparent failure of the French expedition to plan for the conditions they encountered and to respond to the extreme weather when it did occur. The alternative scenario to this is that they were passive to conditions which were within the normal climate regime and were unable or unwilling to recognise the threats and opportunities which the weather presented and to respond appropriately to their own advantage.

The documentary evidence provides little to encourage the view that the weather was exceptional. None of the sources suggest that the easterly gales were so severe as to be the worst within living memory or be described in similar vein, as is frequently recorded in contemporary records when appropriate. Neither Tone, nor military despatches, nor local correspondence, nor later calendars provide such evidence. This is the argument of silence. It becomes more convincing when placed alongside the weather based strategies proposed by Tone when in Brest at the beginning of the expedition. One of these strategies proposed seizing the opportunity that would be presented by an north-easterly gale. This suggests that there was a reasonable expectation of such gales occurring, for why else would Tone contemplate the notion and trouble others with it?

Tone's anticipation of north-easterly gales fits the growing picture that is emerging of some of the aspects of the weather of the eighteenth century. Detailed work on the daily weather of the 1780s shows that the frequency of easterlies was much higher than it is today and was a significant factor in the weather regime, particularly at certain times of the year. The month in which this was most pronounced was December. During the Decembers of 1780–1785 the easterlies were dominant over westerlies.[26] Of course, this may not have been so for

44

a longer period, for long term averages show that westerlies were still important. If Tone and others had their weather memory and expectations shaped by the weather of their earlier years, then it was reasonable for them to have a high expectation of easterly winds during December. For Tone, this certainly appears to have been the case.

These weather conditions have become associated with the Little Ice Age, which, among other features, typically had severe winters.[27] Some winters of the 1790s were among the coldest on record. The coldest January in the Central England Temperature series was 1795, while December 1796 and December 1797 were the coldest Decembers – with 1791 close behind.[28] However, temperatures were not critical to the events that took place in Ireland. Although, had the expedition landed successfully, it is highly likely that they would have become significant; since the troops, already seasick and severely fatigued, with minimal supplies, would have been required to bivouac in the snow and move in very difficult conditions.

WEATHER, POLITICAL OUTCOMES AND MOMENTS OF OPPORTUNITY
In assessing the role of the weather it would be simplistic in the extreme to be deterministic. The weather cannot dictate human action. Nor does the fatalism that such views tend to produce appear appropriate to the analysis of 1796 – a fatalism that would mean that nothing the actors could do would change the outcome. This is clearly not the case as far as this expedition was concerned. Decisions were made which profoundly affected the development of events.

However, the complexities involved in distinguishing the role of numerous factors that contribute to the outcome of events has led to another simplistic type of interpretation. This is to view the weather and climate as a background against which events take place. It is based on treating weather and climate in terms of averages and by the statistics of aggregation. These project the climate as a relatively constant condition of the atmosphere. When expressed in these terms it is difficult to consider the weather as a dynamic factor in the events that shape the outcome of social and political activities. To explore weather as such a dynamic requires the time frame of weather events to match the time frame of particular social and political actions and their outcomes. When this is done the weather is seen to play an active role in the unfolding of history.

This study is concerned with a short term event. Short term individual weather events may play a critical role in key historical situations. To dismiss these as chance is to underestimate the significance of variability as a primary characteristic of climate. These weather events may create moments of opportunity, which may be seized or lost. In this case, such moments of opportunity are able to offset significant advantages of an otherwise superior military or political force.

There were several such moments of opportunity for the French expedition in December 1796. The main one was between 18–21 December, when in crossing the Celtic Sea the dense sea fog provided a cloak of invisibility for most of the French fleet which far outweighed the initial lack of contact between themselves. The relatively stationary, defensive dispositions of the patrolling English vessels kept them in the area covered by dense fog while once the French vessels had passed through the frontal system with which the fog was associated they were able to reassemble with little hindrance off the south coast of Ireland in clear, relatively favourable weather. In particular, the winds were favourable, firstly as easterlies to bring them into position off Mizen Head, and then as north-westerlies to assist their entry into Bantry Bay. But by the time the expedition leaders were prepared to set aside the contingency orders for being separated from the Admiral's vessel, the moment had been lost. A second moment of opportunity may have presented itself on 24 December when the easterly gales abated for a short period. This may have been a moment when the vessels would have been able to move up the bay. But nightfall enticed them into waiting for the next day, when new easterly gales struck. In addition to creating moments of opportunity, the weather also acted directly by severely limiting the choice of actions available to the expedition. In most situations there are a number of options open in response to the weather. But from 21 December onwards, when the series of storms became established (which Wolfe Tone himself had wished for when in Brest!) the range of actions open to the expedition became increasingly fewer. In the end there was an overpowering necessity to abort the expedition, all better options having been closed off by the weather.

AT EVERY STAGE OF THE EXPEDITION the weather was a key factor. However the role of the weather was not a direct one, dictating events and their outcomes. Instead its impact was mediated through the range of opportunities it created combined with the expectations and perceptions of those involved in making critical strategic decisions. Although the weather was mostly treated as an unpredictable variable, Wolfe Tone did try to incorporate it into possible strategies to offset the deficiencies of the expedition. He was probably more aware than others of the opportunities that occurred, but adherence to the rigid military command structure made opportunistic responses very difficult. In the final analysis the sequence of weather events reduced the options available to the French. Wolfe Tone promoted all the options he considered to be open, but admitted at the end of the day that the weather beat him. Detailed analysis of the evidence shows that in terms of the influence of the weather, the Bantry Bay expedition must rank as one of the most significant of European military history.

Acknowledgements
Armagh Observatory kindly made available the daily weather records for December 1796 and January 1797.
The maps were drawn by Michael Murphy. The financial assistance of the Faculty of Arts, UCC, is gratefully acknowledged.

'The Invasion That Never Was'

Naval and Military Aspects of the French Expedition to Bantry Bay, 1796

Thomas Bartlett

During the 1790s, Dublin Castle, the seat of government in Ireland, confronted two 'security' problems: first, with the outbreak of war with revolutionary France in February 1793, it had to see to the defence of Ireland against French incursion; and second, it had to devise policies to combat effectively a growing insurgency problem in the Irish countryside.[1] The central dilemma for Dublin Castle had been that no single security policy could address both problems. On the one hand, the defence of Ireland meant inevitably a concentration of soldiers – along with adequate supplies of tents, biscuits and cattle – at or near the likely invasion sites so that the enemy on landing could be immediately repulsed by a well-equipped force. Moreover, conventional military and naval thinking decreed that a descent on Ireland – if it came at all – would most probably take place on the south coast of Ireland or on the north-east of the island. The east coast of Ireland, with Dublin as its prize, was ruled out on the grounds that no French fleet would run the huge risk of being trapped in the Irish Sea, and then destroyed by the Royal Navy. Similarly, the area on the west and north-west coasts of Ireland, between Galway Bay and Lough Swilly, was in general discounted as a possible location for invasion because of tricky seas, distance from France, and huge supply problems if an army did in fact manage to struggle ashore. Against that, it was well recognised that a concentration of forces played into the hands of the main disturbers of the public peace, the Defenders, a widespread and secret society.

The Defenders had their origins in Armagh in the 1780s but during the 1790s they had spread far beyond that county.[2]

By 1795, Lord Camden the newly-appointed Lord Lieutenant, could list thirteen counties, in south Ulster, north Leinster and north Connacht in which Defenderism had gained a hold. Quite what lay behind Defenderism was something of a mystery: bound up promiscuously with agrarian grievances over tithes, taxes and rents, were found anti-Protestant slogans, millenarian aspirations of a world turned upside-down, and – ominously for Dublin Castle – expressions of support for the French:

> The French Defenders will uphold the cause
> The Irish Defenders will pull down the British Laws.

Moreover, harsh counter-measures to Defenderism – speedy executions, mass arrests, and the shipment of suspects for service in the Royal Navy – had not had the desired effect. Arms raids, killings, robberies had continued unabated throughout 1795–96. It was in these years also that a worrying new development was brought to the attention of Dublin Castle, for reports were received that the Defenders were making common cause with the United Irishmen.

Founded in Belfast in 1791, the Society of United Irishmen had initially sought parliamentary reform by peaceful, constitutional means.[3] However, with the failure of its plan for reform, the outbreak of war with revolutionary France, and especially, the French offer of military assistance to those countries wishing to be free, the United Irishmen had turned their attention to more direct means of achieving their ambitions. In May 1794, following revelations of treasonable contact with the French authorities during the trial of the French agent, the Reverend William Jackson, the Society of United Irishmen was suppressed. This had the unintentional effect of driving out of its ranks the faint-hearted and the half-hearted, and when the society was reconstituted some months later it was as a secret, oath-bound organisation, dedicated to the achievement of an Irish republic with French military assistance. Theobald Wolfe Tone had been involved in briefing Jackson on the situation in Ireland, and he had had to leave Ireland in order to avoid arrest. He had gone to the United States, but he had stayed there only a short time before he took ship for France with the aim of persuading the French authorities of the merits of a full-scale invasion of Ireland. Once in Paris, Tone's views and those of Carnot, the French minister of war, and Hoche, the leading French general of the day, coincided. Tone continually impressed upon the French authorities the huge contribution made by Ireland in men and *matèriel* to the British war effort, and he urged an invasion of Ireland as the surest way of wounding Britain, perhaps fatally. In addition, he stressed the political unreliability of large sections of the armed forces of the crown in Ireland, and he emphasised the emerging alliance between the Defenders and the United Irishmen. Other United Irishmen – Arthur O'Connor, Lord Edward Fitzgerald, Edward Lewins – made similar points in their dealings with the French authorities, and in late 1796 a full-scale invasion was determined upon.[4]

In the eyes of Dublin Castle, however, the main threat to security came not from a French invasion but from rural insurgency associated with the Defenders: the theoretical possibility of a French descent on Ireland was dismissed when set beside the daily record of attacks, assassinations, arms seizures and sectarian brawling throughout large areas of Ireland. Rumours of French interest in an Irish landing were discounted and a policy of counter-insurgency was given precedence over one of defence. Inevitably, this meant a dispersal of forces and the deployment of hundreds of tiny garrisons throughout the disturbed areas. As a result, even though there were frequent rumours that the French were planning some sort of raid on Ireland, there had been few or no preparations to resist the French should they land. This sanguine attitude of Dublin Castle towards a French invasion requires explanation.

In the first instance, the Dublin Castle authorities could call on history in support of their policy of prioritising counter-insurgency over defence, for while there had been many threats of invasion in the eighteenth century, in the end they had all come to nothing.[5] Not since 1689 and 1690 had the French evaded the British squadron protecting Ireland and managed to disembark large numbers of troops. (Thurot's raid of 1759 which had alarmed the citizens of Belfast and Carrick-fergus was just that – a raid, not an invasion.) Moreover, if the French had proved singularly unsuccessful for over a hundred years in mounting a significant expedition to Ireland, there were good reasons for thinking that they could not be any more successful in the years after the outbreak of the French Revolution. It was, in fact, an article of faith that the French navy had noticeably declined in effectiveness since the Revol-ution, for executions, purges, and flight had taken a heavy toll of that navy's most experienced officers. And the British victo-ry on the 'Glorious First of June' [1794] and, even more, the supine surrender of the important naval base at Toulon to the Royal Navy by disaffected members of the French navy had confirmed a comfortable feeling of British naval superiority in contrast to French ineptitude and treason.[6]

Finally, it was axiomatic that seaborne invasions could not be successful without *command of the sea* and this the French palpably did not have and would not have, given the per-ceived chaos into which the French navy had descended since 1793. From an early date in the war, the leading French naval ports had been blockaded, penning up the French sails of the line. By December 1796, Admiral Colpoys with his warships hovered off Brest, while his subordinate, Sir Edward Pellew, in his frigates tacked back and forth in the very mouth of this great natural harbour. Meanwhile at Spithead, sheltered by the Isle of Wight, a large reserve fleet under Admiral Bridport lay at anchor awaiting word of any French attempt to escape the blockade. Finally, off the south coast of Ireland, Admiral Kingsmill with a small squadron was stationed on convoy escort duty.

For these compelling reasons, then, there was little or no fear of a French seaborne invasion: in fact, if anything, there was mounting frustration in naval and political circles that the cowardly French might continue to skulk in their ports and thus elude their fate. Hence, when intelligence was received in the autumn of 1796 that a fleet was being assembled in Brest for an amphibious operation, possibly to Ireland, the hope was that the French would indeed attempt a break-out for this would surely result in the destruction of their fleet and whatever troops it carried. No less a personage than the British Home Secretary, the Duke of Portland, in language no different to that of Wolfe Tone, voiced his own high expectations for a French expedition to Ireland. In November 1796, he frankly declared that he hoped the French would launch an invasion of Ireland 'as it is hardly possible that it could escape the vigilance and superiority of the squadrons which are stationed to observe its motions'.[7] In retrospect, however, it is clear that by this date a healthy confidence with regard to the French threat had yielded to a dangerous complacency: this shift almost brought disaster to the British Empire.

AT THIS POINT IT MAY be convenient to evaluate the forces at the disposal of Dublin Castle in late 1796. In the face of mounting evidence of a Defender–United Irishmen alliance, the Castle had responded uncompromisingly. New laws were put through the Irish Parliament providing for curfews, arrests of suspects and harsh penalties for tendering or taking oaths. *Habeas Corpus* was suspended and provision was made for proclaiming certain districts under military control. An extensive spy network was, with difficulty, set up and by late 1796 Under-Secretary Edward Cooke found himself at the centre of a spider's web of informants, agents, spies and turncoats. Dublin Castle's problem had never been a lack of intelligence, for there had always been a constant flow of reports into the Castle; but rather its difficulty lay in a proper evaluation of the incoming intelligence, and in this respect Cooke's capacity for cool appraisal and dispassionate assessment was vital to the counter-insurgency policies embarked upon in the late 1790s. These new, draconian laws and the Castle's intelligence network, were backed by a huge increase in the range and number of the soldiers available to Dublin Castle.[8] Throughout 1793 an Irish Militia had been embodied. Based on the territorial division of the Irish county, and consisting of Catholic rank and file and (mostly) Protestant officers, these Militia were seen both as a defence force, and also as a sort of nursery for the regular army. There were, however, grave fears as to their reliability; indeed Wolfe Tone in promoting the idea of an invasion of Ireland to the French authorities had argued 'to a moral certainty' that the Militia would desert to the French army when it disembarked in Ireland. In December 1796 there were some 18,000 Militiamen in Ireland.

Alongside the Irish Militia, there were in late 1796 some 9,000 Fencibles. These Fencibles were mostly derived from Scotland and they had arrived in Ireland throughout 1795 in order to facilitate the departure for the West Indian theatre of the regular army regiments then billeted in Ireland. They were unimpressive militarily, being frequently composed of those considered unsuitable for the regular army. As a result of this policy of substituting Fencibles for Regulars, there were only some 3,500 regular cavalry and about 1,600 regular infantry in Ireland in late 1796. The demands of the West Indian theatre had been remorseless and this explains the small numbers of regulars in Ireland at the end of the year.

In addition to the above, there was the recently embodied Yeomanry armament. Approval for the setting up of a Yeomanry had been grudgingly given by Dublin Castle in September 1796 and there had been a rush to form both cavalry and infantry corps. The duties of the Yeomanry were to police 'their' counties and, in the event of an invasion, to assist the Militia, Fencibles and Regulars by keeping an eye on the (allegedly) disaffected within their areas. Such people, it was felt, might think to take advantage of the alarm and stage diversionary attacks. The Yeomanry, contrary to received opinion, was not an exclusively Protestant, much less Orange force: but it was disproportionately recruited in Ulster and in that province, it rapidly acquired a reputation for militant loyalism; this notoriety soon infused the whole. By December 1796, there might have been some 20,000 Yeomanry, but they were new, untried and not yet fully equipped.

These forces, in total some 53,000, were divided into five districts, approximating to northern, southern, eastern, western, and central, and they were under the overall command of Lord Carhampton, latterly infamous for his dragooning of Connacht in late 1795.

Some general points may be made about these armed forces of the crown. First, as noted above, they were widely dispersed; there were important garrisons only at Blaris, near Belfast and at Loughlinstown, near Dublin. If the French could successfully disembark a sizeable force, it would take many days to mobilise an army capable of opposing it.[9] Second, widespread dispersal of the soldiers had had a bad effect – it was generally agreed – on discipline. Frequently, the men were billeted beyond the control of an officer, and often they were encouraged to go beyond what the law would permit in pursuit of rural insurgents. Moreover, as a result of slack discipline, a number of the Militia regiments in particular had been infiltrated by both the United Irishmen and the Defenders.[10] Third, there was much criticism both of the officers in the Irish regiments, and of the more senior regular army officers. Many of the Irish officers were absentees who often owed their appointments to political influence, while regular staff officers were held to be generally uninspiring, barely adequate to prosecute counter-insurgency policies and mostly too incompetent to serve elsewhere. The threatened French landing at Bantry Bay in late December 1796 would prove a real test of the crown's armed forces.

HUGH GOUGH HAS ALREADY DESCRIBED the misadventures which befell the French fleet that sailed from Brest; but a number of observations may, none the less, be made.[11] First, the French fleet did in fact arrive off Bantry Bay, though not all of the warships and troop carriers did so at the same time. Fatally for the success of the mission, however, the *Fraternité* with both the military and naval commanders – Hoche and Morard de Galles, respectively – on board, never arrived at all. Second, the foul weather cannot bear all or even most of the responsibility for the failure of the expedition. Wolfe Tone's despairing comment that 'notwithstanding all our blunders, it is the dreadful stormy weather and easterly winds which have been blowing furiously and without intermission since we made Bantry Bay that have ruined us' cannot be accepted without challenge.[12] The reality was that the poor weather conditions were an asset not a hindrance to the French: the storms had facilitated the French escape from Brest; they had prevented an informed pursuit by the blockade fleet; they had held up the dispatch of the vital intelligence of the French departure getting to the Admiralty; they had helped delay Admiral Bridport's departure from Spithead; lastly they had allowed the French fleet to return unchallenged to its home port. Moreover, in the three weeks during which the French fleet, or elements of it, had been tossed about in or off Bantry Bay, no fewer than three 'weather windows' had briefly opened in any one of which a disembarkation might have been attempted. None was: and it may be suggested that poor seamanship and inept leadership (the absence of the charismatic Hoche was surely crucial in this respect) led to the expedition being abandoned *re infecta*.

How had the Royal Navy conducted itself in this emergency? It is sometimes forgotten that in examining the Bantry Bay expedition we are dealing with two, if not three, failures. Obviously, the French failed to land: but the British failed to be forewarned and, crucially, they failed to intercept the French either going to or returning from Ireland. The intelligence failure on the part of the British lies beyond the scope of this paper: but the French fleet did after all return to Brest, and the majority of the French ships had not sighted an English sail during their voyage. How can this failure be explained?

Sir Edward Pellew in his frigate off the mouth of Brest did see the French leave, but because of poor visibility he was unable to contact Admiral Colpoys and the main blockade squadron. Moreover, Pellew strongly suspected that Portugal was the intended destination. The result was that Colpoys only learned of the French departure on 24 December, but because he was unsure of their destination – he too suspected Portugal – he decided to continue off Brest. A solitary frigate was dispatched to Portugal to confirm the direction of the French fleet. By the time Colpoys realised his mistake, he and his ships were caught up in the complex easterlies, and he failed to make contact with other British ships off the Lizard, and instead was forced to make for Spithead. News of the French arrival at

Bantry had in fact pre-dated Colpoys and on 22 December, Admiral Bridport had been ordered to make sail 'immediately' for Brest to confirm the French fleet's departure, and then to head for Cape Clear. On 24 December this order was countermanded and he was ordered to sail directly to Cape Clear. Bridport was unable to complete his fleet until 25 December; there was then a delay after two ships collided and one ran aground; contrary winds on 26 and 27 December produced further delay and it was not until 3 January that Bridport finally sailed – to Brest and then to Ireland – where he arrived too late to intercept the French.[13]

This sorry catalogue of error, miscalculation, and sheer ineptitude stemmed directly from an overweening confidence in British naval superiority and a wholly misplaced conviction of the efficacy of the blockade system as currently practised. Astonishingly, although Admiral Richery and his commerce raiders had escaped out of Rochefort in early 1796, sailed to Newfoundland, plundered British possessions there and sailed back in triumph, no lessons had been learned by the Admiralty. Colpoys' conduct off Brest is inexplicable: it certainly looked as if he had no stomach for a fight with the French. And Bridport's lacklustre performance at Spithead ought not to be overlooked; it had taken him three weeks to sail 'immediately'; he was found to be in contravention of standing orders in that he resided many miles inland from the port; and there were too many ships in reserve and not enough deployed in the blockade (though this was not Bridport's fault). In the end, however, behind the British muddle and incompetence lay the mindset which simply could not believe that the French would make a winter descent on Ireland. Such hubris might nearly have led to nemesis.

> Oh where was Hood and where was Howe
> And where Cornwallis then
> Where was Colpoys, Bridport or Pellew
> And all their gallant men?

IF THE NAVAL RESPONSE TO the emergency posed by the breakout of the French fleet was unimpressive, the reaction of the land forces was both inept and chaotic. While there had been some discussion in the latter half of 1796 concerning preparations for resisting an invasion, little if anything had in fact been done. Priority, as we have seen, was accorded to counter-insurgency, and as a result there were no large troop encampments on or near the south coast, or indeed anywhere outside Dublin or Belfast. It was unforgivable that the minimum measures called for in the various military plans – the construction of supply depots at Waterford, Clonmel, Cork, Bandon, Limerick and Galway, or the setting up of communication beacons – had not in fact been undertaken. Consequently, even if a large force had been assembled to repulse the French, it was unclear how this force would have been fed. On this basis alone, if Cork had fallen to the French – and this would surely have solved all *their* supply problems – it might have been months before a fully-equipped force could have challenged the French in Munster.

Moreover, just as a chain of communication beacons had not been set up, so too there was no direct communication between Lord Camden in Dublin Castle and Admiral Kingsmill on board ship off the south coast of Ireland. Camden had in fact invited Kingsmill to Dublin Castle in September 1796 to discuss defence matters: but Kingsmill had ignored him. There may have been an Irish army, but there was no Irish navy, and Kingsmill answered to the Admiralty in London, not to Dublin Castle. Thus, when the French arrived off Bantry, Kingsmill saw no reason to keep Camden informed. On 26 December, Camden wrote to Kingsmill complaining of his disappointment at being kept in the dark concerning the French, at not having 'the opinion of professional men of high rank' on this crisis. He also wrote to Earl Spencer at the Admiralty denouncing Kingsmill's 'total silence'. In point of fact, Camden was kept well informed by his man on the spot, Major Brown of the Engineers: but none the less, the lack of information from Kingsmill was galling.

On 26 December 1796, Camden revealed his ponderous thought processes to his uninspiring Commander-in-Chief, Carhampton: he informed him that, taking into account intelligence received from General Dalrymple in Cork, the opinion of Captain Boyle of the Royal Navy, observations from other witnesses (including Major Brown), and confirmation that the French had indeed sailed out of Brest harbour, he had reached a conclusion. These circumstances, he wrote, 'leave me no room to doubt of the Fleet which has for some days appeared off Bantry Bay being hostile'. Carhampton was ordered to mobilise an adequate force to march against the French should they land: revealingly, he was instructed not to command it himself but instead to remain in Dublin where he was needed.

Accordingly, three columns were got ready under Generals Eustace, Crosbie and Dundas on the evening of 26 December: on account of the 'severity of the weather, the suddenness of the march and the inexperience of the troops' the men were issued with extra rations and a liberal quantity of spirits. A day later, however, after the troops had struggled south in appalling conditions, Carhampton concluded that there was now no danger of a French landing at Bantry and he sent dispatches ordering his columns to halt: Crosbie at Kilkenny, Eustace at Cashel, and Dundas at Roscrea. Carhampton was worried that the French, thwarted at Bantry Bay, might sail further along the south-west coast of Ireland and either attempt a landing at the mouth of the Shannon, and make for Limerick, or disembark in Galway Bay, possibly at the town of Galway itself. Hence his columns, poised to move west or south-west or even south to Cork, were now to await the next French move.

In reality, despite this orderly disposition on paper, on the ground the military response was at sixes and sevens. It was evident that Cork – with its huge quantity of provisions, and its symbolic importance – would have been abandoned. The three columns mobilised by Carhampton scarcely mustered 9,000 troops between them and they would surely have proved no match for 15,000 French veterans 'chosen men, clothed in scarlet' led by the charismatic Hoche.[14] In addition, and an added worry for Dublin Castle, there were some 1,600 French prisoners of war in the Cork area; and it was assumed that they would make common cause with the enemy. In

Limerick, the troops had scrambled to meet a possible French threat: General Charles Vallancey on duty with the Militia wrote to a correspondent: 'I cannot give you any account of the confusion that reigned there [Limerick]'.[15] Lord Castlereagh, at the head of the Derry Militia marching from Limerick to Cork, noted that 'Mr Whiskey' had done some damage to the men's discipline but it was the contradictory orders from Generals Dalrymple and Smith that most infuriated him.[16] The former was elderly and very overweight, and had proved unenergetic in his previous posting in the sectarian cockpit of Armagh. In preparing for his march to Bandon, the priority he had given to his personal supply of cayenne pepper and capers caused murmurings amongst his subordinates, and observers. A local magnate, Lord Longueville, commented in a letter to Dublin Castle that the generals in the Munster area 'are not worth a rap halfpenny', and he reported that when 'Dalrymple had a fit at Dunmanway and fell off his chair, the people under his command were sorry he recovered'. Dublin Castle itself received reports from various quarters of generals abandoning their men and seeking comfortable billets for themselves.[17] None the less, for all the toing and froing, the incompetence and the lack of preparation, Ireland did not experience an invasion, and the French sailed away. What lessons, if any, were drawn from the whole episode, and wherein lies the significance of 'the invasion that never was'?

WITH CONFIRMATION OF THE DEPARTURE of the French, Camden's Chief Secretary, Thomas Pelham, argued that it was now 'time to reflect on what has passed and, like mariners after a storm, we should lose no time in examining our vessel, stopping all leaks and, I believe, putting in new timbers.'[18] An inquest was got under way immediately, and initially turned up some encouraging findings. 'Providence,' noted Lord Clare, 'has befriended us'; it had been 'a Providential deliverance' claimed Camden. Not for the first time a 'Protestant wind' had saved Ireland: and this was of course reassuring, as was further confirmation of French ineptitude and poor seamanship.[19] In addition, while it was acknowledged that the overall military response to the emergency had been less than satisfactory, there was general agreement that the one unequivocal success had been the performance of the newly-constituted Irish Yeomanry. Yeomanry corps had mobilised swiftly and taken over garrison duties, while their officers – 'men of three and four thousand pounds a year' – had not felt it beneath their dignity to carry expresses or escort baggage trains.[20] Finally, the country had stayed peaceful; the Catholic bishops had behaved splendidly (Dr Moylan of Cork was especially mentioned), and in the south of Ireland there were very positive signs of the loyalty of the people.[21] Camden recorded that local inhabitants had cleared snow out of the way of troops on their march, and had even shared their meagre provisions with them. At Carlow, a subscription had been taken up for the troops, and at Limerick and Cork they were given assistance in transporting their artillery. 'In short,' concluded Camden, 'the general disposition of the people through the south and west was so prevalent that I have no doubt had the enemy landed their hope of assistance would have been totally disappointed.'[22] These things apart, however, there was precious little public reason for self-congratulation: and even the display of loyalty was privately pooh-poohed. 'Had a complete landing been effected,' noted Cooke, 'I fear that there would have been another tale';[23] and General Dalyrmple in his report on the emergency wrote: 'While our Eagles head to the enemy, the people will probably act with us: turn your standards,' he scoffed, 'and they will probably turn with them'.[24] It was, however, the sullen response from the north of Ireland, and from Belfast especially, which gave greatest concern, for while the rest of Ireland had displayed at least outward loyalty, these areas had not.

So 'very alarming' had been the reports from his northern informants that Camden could not bring himself to order troops from Ulster to join the columns marching against the French: Pelham explained that 'the disaffection of the inhabitants of the north ... made it necessary to consider the troops in that district as a separate army'.[25] On receipt of news of the French arrival off Bantry, Pelham had immediately ordered the destruction of the *Northern Star*, the United Irishmen's news-paper published in Belfast, if the French should effect a land-ing.[26] But a more measured and draconian response came after the French had returned to Brest. Camden had promised to take 'severe steps' against the north and, early in the new year, General Lake was ordered to take an army and disarm that province. Lake was given 'discretionary orders' which in effect meant, so Camden explained, 'that he was not to suffer the cause of justice to be frustrated by the delicacy which might possibly have actuated the magistracy'.[27] Portland had earlier baulked at the severity of the punishments prescribed in the Insurrection Act (1796) but now, reeling from the near-run thing of a French invasion, he expressed his hearty approval of these repressive measures. 'There is little distinction,' he remarked grimly, 'to be made between indifference and disaf-fection'.[28] In the wake of Bantry Bay, an onslaught was un-leashed against the United Irishmen in Ulster: 'The govern-ment,' wrote Camden, 'meant to strike terror'.[29]

The dragooning of Ulster was one response to the disaf-fection displayed during the invasion scare; another was a firm resolve to render the armed forces more efficient and to purge them of disloyal elements. The French had clearly counted on rogue elements particularly within the Irish Militia to turn their coats and join them. When Joseph Harvey, a seaman who was picked up by the French and subsequently released, underwent interrogation on his return to Bantry, he revealed that the French 'expect the Militia in their favour'; but this rev-elation came as no surprise, for Dublin Castle was already well aware of attempts made to suborn members of the armed forces of the crown.[30] The Bantry Bay emergency, however, prompted a flurry of orders, inquiries and eventually courts martial which resulted within months in the execution of around twenty soldiers and the departure abroad of scores of others. The army generals, too, came under scrutiny in the wake of Bantry Bay; and their performance was assessed as unsatisfactory. Within months, General Stewart, suffering from a stroke and judged 'perfectly useless' by Camden, was forced out; General Amherst, dubbed a 'mad Methodist' by Clare, and accused of uttering 'some very questionable language' by his fellow officers, went soon after; and General Dalrymple, whose shrewd military mind was belied by his appearance, was quickly retired.[31] Even the commander-in-chief, Car-hampton, did not escape. Camden had never had confidence in him, and had only recommended him for the post some four months earlier because there was no one else: he now became perhaps the most notable casualty of the French expedition to Bantry Bay. Camden was able to dispense with Carhampton's services because he knew he would have no trouble getting someone better. Ironically, so long as Ireland had been associ-ated only with boring garrison duty and aiding the civil authorities, the best generals had shunned that station. The threatened French invasion – and the prospect that the French would return – changed all that. Ireland was now a theatre of war where reputation, honour and glory could be won: it could be an Italy in the west for some hungry British general. Lord Cornwallis, a veteran of America and India, was ap-proached, but it was General Ralph Abercromby, 'entre nous, one of the best if not on the whole the very best officers in the King's service', who took up the challenge.[32] He set out to rebuild the Irish army, to impose discipline on it and to put it firmly under military control. His efforts in these respects led to a clash with Dublin Castle, and following his famous 'General Orders' of February 1798 in which he denounced the discipline of the forces under his command, he had no choice but to resign. His departure was the signal for increased mili-tary repression which within months had triggered the insur-rection of 1798.

The Royal Navy, too, conducted an examination into its performance in the crisis which, perhaps predictably, exoner-ated itself from all blame. Its failure to intercept the French was excused because 'the state of the information ... tho' it had been reported that the enemy had meditated a descent on Ireland, rather led to a belief that their real operations were likely to be directed to the coast of Portugal'.[33] The trenchant criticism voiced in the British Parliament was robustly rejected; and Lord Spencer of the Admiralty even found time to protest to

Camden at the lack of recognition accorded the Royal Navy's role in the Irish Parliament's debate on the threatened invasion.[34] Clearly, Bantry Bay was not going to produce a Byng *pour encourager les autres;* and yet, for all the public defence of the Royal Navy's actions, certain lessons had in fact been learnt about the efficacy of the current blockading practice and these were put into effect, unobtrusively, later in 1797.

Colpoys was soon sidelined: officially because of his uninspired handling of the naval mutiny at the Nore some months later, but there were suspicions that his lacklustre display off Brest may have had something to do with it. Again, Admiral Bridport may have received official backing in the weeks after Bantry Bay, but within months, he was replaced by Lord St Vincent who renewed the blockade system by organising a rotation of duty to keep the captains on their toes, and by committing a much larger share of the reserve fleet to blockade duty.[35] Bridport had failed to recognise that no naval battle was ever won from the harbour; and it was St Vincent's tactics which kept the French penned in their ports until their fleet was destroyed at Trafalgar in 1805.

In the end, perhaps the most important lesson of the whole episode of the French descent on Bantry, was that drawn by Irish loyalists. Dublin Castle had let them down; British intelligence had failed them; the Royal Navy had not protected them; and the generals and the admirals had been uninspiring. Only the Yeomanry, their force, had performed creditably: once again Irish loyalists had learnt that they could only rely on themselves alone; and this attitude was very evident in the 1798 rebellion. Perhaps the real significance of the 'invasion that never was' lies here?

1. Letter from Major John Brown, Cove Fort, 22 December 1796 to Lord Camden, Dublin (Kent Archives Office [hereafter KAO], Pratt Papers, U840/0170/1)

My Lord,
I did not think it necessary to trouble your excellency on the last alarm as I know you had earlier and better information from the Admiral [Kingsmill] than I could give of the nature of the squadron said to be French. They are now known to be part of Admiral Mann's squadron of which Admiral Kingsmill had an express last night, as also information of one of his cruizers having captured a privateer.

I have no news of any sort to send your excellency. There is only one frigate in the harbour. All the others are out to the westward, one or two is expected in today and the *Kangeroo* tomorrow.

I have been much hurried since I came here and hope soon to reduce the enormous expense and establishment here in our department. The impositions of every sort which are practiced are beyond belief and the extravagant wages which has been given to tradesmen and labourers seems only to have increased idleness and peculation.

The severe frost has been so unfavourable that I have closed off all the posts except Fort Camden which was in so defenceless a state that I must go on for some time patching up the old work in a temporary way until the [Barrack] Board fix on a proper plan which I shall lay before them when I go to Dublin and am not without hopes of winding up the business here so as to be able to accomplish this before the winter be over. I am, etc.

2. Letter from Brown, Cork to Camden, Dublin, 4 o'clock p.m. 23 December 1796 (KAO, U840/0170/2)

[No salutation]
I came here this morning in consequence of the alarm which your excellency is already acquainted with. No intelligence has arrived from Bantry since morning and although every step is taking here to oppose the enemy yet in general it is not believed and this morning I saw the Admiral [Kingsmill] who is clearly of opinion that they can-

not be French as the wind we have had for some days past would not have brought them here. He says it may probably be the Lisbon or Quebec convoy or possibly Sir John Jervis from the Mediterranean whom Admiral Mann when spoke to by one of Admiral Kingsmill's squadron some days ago off Cape Clear seemed to expect.

The Galway Militia [three words too faint to read] and the Waterford Regiment has marched forward together with four light six p[ounder]s to Bandon and Dunmanway, and orders are issued should they prove to be enemies, to drive the cattle, [and] destroy and lay waste the country so as to render their approach to this city [Cork] as difficult as possible and I am in hopes they may be opposed till the troops of the country arrive to our assistance.

The Yeomanry corps here are extremely alert and useful and this town seems extremely loyal. 1,200 men this night will be at Bandon and in the course of tomorrow about 4,000 will be collected towards Bandon and Dunmanway; the Light companies are to advance towards Dunmanway in the morning accompanied by the Artillery. Should this prove a false alarm it will have a good effect of shewing the alacrity of the people and the great want of preparations for these rapid movements.

7 o'clock: Captain Cotter who was sent forward to Bantry this morning has this moment sent an express from Drumaleague where he met Mr White [fleeing] from Bantry with his family. This express contains nothing [definite?] except that a fleet of 25 sail of large ships are actually beating into Bantry Bay. The Admiral is still positive they cannot be French; the accounts hitherto are positive and in some degree contradictory. The boats which have been sent from Bantry for intelligence have all been detained which looks ill.

I am ashamed to send you this but if you knew our hurry and confusion you would excuse me. I am, etc.

3. Letter from Brown to Camden, 1 o'clock Saturday morning, 24th December [1796] (KAO, U840/0170/3)

My Lord,
By an express this moment to the Admiral dated at sea 22nd [December] there seems to be little doubt that the fleet seen in Bantry Bay are French. Captain Boyle who forwards the express has proceeded to England to acquaint the Admiralty. The troops are all in motion and the wind being unfavourable for them – the enemy – to get up into Bantry Bay, I hope time will be given to get possession of the strong posts before they can land. It is said that some of them are

actually in Bearhaven but the country is so strong and roads so bad from there to Bantry I scarcely think they will attempt landing there but push for Bantry. I am, etc.

[Postscript]
The Admiral is here and would have written to your excellency but has no information except what the General's [i.e., Dalrymple] despatches contain. Tomorrow I am to be sent forward with the troops. J.B.

4. Letter from Brown, Bandon, to Camden, Dublin, 6 o'clock p.m., 24 [December, 1796]

[No salutation]
I proceeded here with General Dalrymple and on our arrival met an express from Mr White of Bantry which left that place this morning at 3 o'clock. He had the evening before counted the fleet and positively affirms that they amount in all to 60 ships, from 13 to 17 of the line. They were then beating in the mouth of Bantry Bay with a contrary wind. Mr White adds that he had accounts of 6 sail of English men of war being in Crookhaven. He sent an express to warn them of their danger.

An officer has this moment arrived from Dunmanway. He says at four o'clock this afternoon he left that place and before he left it he saw a gentleman who left Bantry this morning at nine o'clock and the fleet were still beating, that at Dunmanway they heard a heavy firing: God send it may be the British fleet. The express is just going. I proceed tomorrow to Bantry. I am, etc.

5. Letter from Brown, Dunmanway to Camden, Dublin, 10 o'clock p.m. 25 December 1796 (KAO, U840/0170/5)

My Lord,
The latest and most correct account from Bantry arrived here this moment from Lt. Pelling of the navy dated 4 o'clock this afternoon, says the fleet came to anchor at 6 o'clock last night off Bearhaven. They consist altogether of 17 sail, 8 of which are two-deckers, the rest are frigates, luggars and some large vessels he could not distinguish whether men of war or not. It therefore appears that the greater part has been blown off and are now out of sight of this part of the coast. It blows now extremely fresh and has done so since last night a little to the south of east. If I was to presume to give an opinion, I should

think them in a most unpleasant and highly dangerous situation.

I have attended General Dalrymple here and am very anxious to get on to see the situation of this fleet. Both Generals Coote and Dalrymple are here and mean to proceed to Bantry tomorrow morning, but we travel slow.

May I presume to be mentioned to Lady Camden and to wish you all a merry Christmas being convinced that you have little to fear from any attack here. While this weather lasts everything is against them. It is intensely cold and so hard is the frost that travelling is very difficult. I am, etc.

6. *Letter from Brown, Bantry, to Camden, Dublin, 2 o'clock p.m., Monday 26 December [1796] enclosing a memorandum of a conversation with Mr White and Lieutenant Pelling R.N. (KAO, U840/0170/6)*

My Lord,
The above memorandum contains the substance of a great deal of conversation I have had with Mr White and Lt. Pelling of the navy who was sent by Admiral Kingsmill in a cutter but proceeded here from Castlehaven by land. He is now here and is clearly of opinion that no fleet on earth could have rode out the late stormy weather in 40 fathom water as they were. A messenger is this moment arrived who is a confidential servant of Mr White's: he says they are positively sailed and that he had a good view of the place where they were anchored yesterday but no ship was to be seen.

The day is very hazy and of course he could not see four [sic]. If they are all gone which scarcely admits of a doubt, they must have slipped their cables in the night; the last guns they fired as signal was about 10 o'clock. It continues to blow quite a storm accompanied with rain and heavy sleet. Generals Coote and Dalrymple are here.

Lt. Pelling thinks they must be blown off the coast as they can make no part of Ireland, and while the wind remains in this point they cannot return to their own country. It may appear to your excellency that I should have gone to the spot where this fleet lay to satisfy myself whether they were really gone or not but the weather is so hazy I could not see two miles and I am in such a situation as barely to be able to write from cold, riding [i.e., having ridden] from Dunmanway the worst day I ever was out in, and as they lay about 7 leagues from this place by the worst road in Ireland it would be impossible for me to do it this night. Tomorrow morning if the weather clears I shall. I am, etc.

Since I wrote the above a Mr O'Sullivan has come in here from Bear-haven with a French officer a prisoner who with six men was drove ashore near the Dursay islands last Saturday. The generals are now examining him and of course will send better information than I can. He has said to Mr O'Sullivan that the French fleet consisted of fifty sail, 25 of which were of the line, that Richery commanded a squadron and that General Hoche commanded the troops consisting of 25,000 men. Mr O'Sullivan whom I have conversed with positively says that he left Bearhaven this day at one o'clock and that he then saw part of the fleet at anchor and that he supposes the weather prevented him seeing the rest.

When I wrote the first part of this letter, I thought the general on his arrival would have sent off an express. It is now exactly twelve o'clock at night.

[Enclosure]
Wednesday the 21st, Mr Bailey's first express from Bearhaven acquainting Mr White of his having discovered and reckoned 23 sail of large ships, three or four brigs and two luggars off the Dursays standing S.S.E. This intelligence left Bantry at 10 o'clock.

Thursday 22nd, Mr White having heard that a fleet was off Dunmanway Bay went to see them and clearly saw seven sail standing for Bantry Bay. On Mr White's return, an express arrived from Mr O'Sullivan of Bearhaven stating that a French fleet was beating up Bantry Bay, a letter from Mr Bayley to the same purport and an affidavit of three men who swore they were taken by the French fleet and escaped in the night leaving some of their boat's crew on board. This intelligence was sent from Bantry at 5 o'clock, Thursday evening.

Friday the 23rd., Mr White saw a fleet and a sail [sic] in the Bay consisting of seventeen sail; at the same time received a third express from Mr Bayley saying they were French to a certainty. They came to anchor off Bear Island in the evening.

Saturday the 24th., Information from Lt. Pelling: the fleet got under way and continued working till night under an [easie?] sail which is a proof they had no intention of coming far up the Bay. At night they anchored again off Bear Island: at this time they consisted of eight two-decked ships, two frigates, two luggars and two brigs and three ships too far of two say whether ships of the line or frigates.

Sunday, they remained all day at anchor and were viewed by Lt. Pelling of the Navy at the distance of about 3 miles at 2 o'clock p.m., when he made the above observation as to their strength. Saturday night and Sunday all say it continued to blow hard, east a little to the south, and Sunday it increased to a storm.

7. Letter from Brown, Bantry, to Camden, Dublin, 3 o'clock p.m. 27 December 1796 (KAO, U840/0170/7)

My Lord,
I am this moment returned from having seen the French fleet at anchor in the mouth of this Bay. They stretch from Bear Island towards Sheeps Head and I counted through the haze seven large ships and three smaller. They were between me and the Bear Island, I mean the three smaller ships, and as I thought very near the shore. I have little doubt that all seen yesterday being seventeen are still at anchor. Last night and all this morning it blew very hard and the heaviest rain I ever saw. It is now clear and fine with the wind to the southward. It is nearly high water and it is thought they will not weigh anchor this night except it may be to endeavour to clear the [lines?].

I have proposed to the General [Dalrymple] to go in a row boat and to get as near as possible to ascertain as much as is in my power their force, but the sailors here say it is impossible. If the sea falls by morning I shall certainly attempt it.

Twelve sail of large ships were seen yesterday off the Dursey Islands, supposed to be part of the enemy's fleet. The generals remain here this night which seems to me rather imprudent as they are certainly in some degree of danger of being carried off. It blows hard now and has every appearance of increasing. It is at S.E and by E., changed since I began this letter. I am, etc.

8. Letter from Brown, Bantry, to Camden, Dublin, 12 o'clock at night, 27 December 1796 (KAO, U840/1070/8)

My Lord,
I wrote you some hours ago but as I understand since it only goes as far as Cork by express, this may probably reach you sooner, and I shall repeat nearly the substance of it.

At two o'clock this day, it cleared for about an hour and I had just time to view the French fleet now at anchor in the mouth of this Bay. I saw distinctly ten ships, 7 of which were very large between Sheep Head and Bear Island and it appeared to me that three of those were very near the Bear Island shore. Nothing has since been heard of them and it is beyond the comprehension of all the seafaring people here how it is possible for them to ride out such a severe gale as has blown for several days. They ride in an exposed place in 40 fathoms of water and at this moment it blows harder than ever. If our own fleet be safe, I hope we have little to fear.

Twelve sail of the enemy were seen yesterday off the Dursey Islands; they must now be blown off, and I am convinced nothing induces the French fleet to lye where they now are but the fear of being drove into the western ocean, crowded with troops and probably short of water and provisions.

The generals return tomorrow to Bandon and I am directed to accompany them. A Mr [Puxley?] set off this night for Bearhaven and has offered very handsomely to go out at all risques to go out in a small cutter to view the fleet and carry intelligence to the British admiral if he can be found.

It blows now a perfect hurricane and rains excessively from the S. S. E. I am convinced there is an end to this expedition. If it be possible I will endeavour to go and get another sight of the fleet before we return. I am, etc.

9. Letter from Brown, Bantry, to Camden, Dublin, 1 o'clock p.m., 29 December 1796 (KAO, U840/0170/9)

My Lord,
Last night I wrote you a few lines, since then nothing has occurred here. It blew pretty hard at south all night and this morning blows (and looks very stormy) from the west, southwest accompanied by heavy rain and very [?great] haze.

Sir James Duff arrived here late last [?night] and returns this day to Mallow. I believe General Dalrymple and Coote remain here. They are in good quarters and *very comfortable.* I understand the troops are stopped till farther orders. The only object the French can have now is to get back as it is totally impossible they can unite in sufficient force in this stormy weather. In haste, I am, etc.

10. Letter from Brown, Bantry, to Camden, Dublin, 10 o'clock a.m. 1 January 1797 (KAO, U840/0170/10)

My Lord,
About three o'clock yesterday afternoon two large launches came from the enemy's ships (with about 80 men in each) round the west end of Whiddy Island. One of them boarded an Amercian Brig opposite to Mr White's house, took away her mate and papers and returned by the east end of the island to their ships. They kept sound-

ing as they went along.

During the night the enemy was joined by another frigate. They now consist of two 74-gun ships, four frigates and a luggar, and two large ships are this minute discovered in the mouth of the Bay outside Bearhaven. I hope Admiral Elphinstone who sailed yesterday from Crookhaven with the intention of looking into this Bay [sic]. He is a fortunate man and I think the enemy's ships here will make little resistance. The enemy show no sign of quitting this station. What little wind there is, is from the north.

Some men who had boarded the enemy on their first appearance here were yesterday set on shore. They report the enemy to be crowded with troops commanded by General Lee, an Irishman from this part of the country who was uncommonly civil to them. They also add that that part of the fleet which first made this harbour has not been seen or heard of by those now here and that they ran in here expecting to meet their admiral and fleet.

I begin now to think they will not attempt to land except joined by the rest of their fleet, as yesterday all day and this morning has been extremely favourable for that purpose [if they] had any such intention.

I wish your excellency and Lady Camden many happy returns of the season and I am, etc.

11. Letter from Brown, Bantry, to Camden, Dublin, 11 o'clock a.m. 2 January 1797 (KAO, U840/0170/11)

My Lord,
The enemy's ships to the north of Whiddy Island remain stationed exactly in the same manner as I mentioned yesterday nor have they shown any disposition to land.

About 12 o'clock yesterday a line of battle ship came from the westward and anchored off the east end of Bear Island and in the dusk of the evening one line of battle ship and one frigate preceded by a cutter came from the southward round Sheep Head which I am in hopes is Admiral Elphinstone and *Diana*, frigate. The line of battle ship, supposed to be Admiral El., during the night cast anchor near the south shore within Sheep's Head point and the cutter continued plying between her and the line of battle ship near the east point of Bear Island, possibly the *Polyphemus*, which convinces me they are both friends or both enemies.

The wind is now S.E. and perfectly fair for the British fleet to come to our assistance. The French might have got out off this Bay yesterday if they had chose it, and this day also, but they seem perfectly inactive, nor are they in a disposition or line so as to make a defence should our fleet appear. The French luggar is cruizing about half way between Bear Island and Whiddy. We have now here about 500 men but the landing places are so extensive that little opposition can be made should they be disposed to land in force. We have reports of several large ships being seen to the southward of Sheep's Head point at a great distance. I am just going out to look on Whiddy Island. I believe nothing but what I see but it is not improbable that this may be the van of the British fleet. I am, etc.

12. Letter from Brown, Bantry, to Camden, Dublin, 6 o'clock p.m. 3 January 1797 (KAO, U840/0170/12)

My Lord,
The ships which sailed from here last night are, as I am informed, come to anchor off Bearhaven. The weather has been so hazy and so very stormy that although I have been looking out all day from Whiddy Island, I could only see two frigates, one off the west end of Whiddy Island and the other under the north shore. I could plainly see the top mast of the frigate which they scuttled and sank last night* and observed the frigate off the west and off Whiddy drive nearly two miles from her anchors; where she brought up is said to be rocky ground and should the gale increase she must be dashed to pieces on the north shore opposite to Whiddy Island.

The wind is at south, one point to the west, blows hard with heavy rain and seems increasing. There is little doubt the way the wind has been all last night and this day that all the ships seen yesterday must still be in some part of this Bay and certainly in a most deplorable situation.

I am this night relieved by a Major Conway and have received orders to join General Dal[rymple] at Bandon which I do tomorrow morning. I am, etc.

The centrepiece of the French Armada exhibition in Bantry House is a 1 to 6 scale model of this frigate, the Surveillante, *which lies 100 feet beneath the sea in Bantry Bay and which has been designated a national monument.*

'IN THE SERVICE OF THE FRENCH REPUBLIC'?

WOLFE TONE IN BANTRY BAY

TOM DUNNE

The aborted French expedition to Ireland in December 1796 represents, perhaps, the most intriguing 'might-have-been' of modern Irish history. The presence on one of the ships that reached Bantry Bay of the romantic figure of Theobald Wolfe Tone, putative father of Irish nationalism, in the uniform of a French officer, has tended to condition our view of the expedition as one designed to liberate Ireland from English rule, and to encourage speculation on its likely outcome in those terms. However, the reality of a successful landing might have been very different and Tone himself had major concerns about French motivation, and about the danger that success might mean further expansion of the French empire rather than Irish independence. His journals for the previous year also suggest that he had himself become sufficiently imbued with the growing militarism and imperialism of French political culture to make his views on such an outcome surprisingly mixed.[1]

Fourteen years ago an essay of mine on Tone's political philosophy was published as a little paperback by the late and much-missed Seán Daly of Tower Books, under the somewhat provocative title, *Theobald Wolfe Tone: colonial outsider*. Seven years later it was mentioned by Brendan Bradshaw in his seminal anti-revisionist article, 'Nationalism and historical scholarship in Ireland', as an example of the 'invincible scepticism' informing what he considered a politically motivated 'revision' of the nationalist interpretation of Irish history. This sought to reduce 'national heroes' like Tone to the status of mere mortals, motivated by class interests and confused intellectually. In a much appreciated backhanded compliment, he described my argument as 'all the more insidious for the elegance of the treatment'. A much greater, if unintended, compliment was paid it two years later with the appearance of Marianne Elliott's monumental biography, *Wolfe Tone: Prophet of Irish independence.* While rather dismissive of my efforts, Professor Elliott basically confirmed my argument about Tone's ideology, and in particular the limited nature of his radicalism and the relatively unformed development of his nationalism. This excellent biography contains much new detail about Tone and the contexts in which his thinking developed, particularly the French. Elliott's study and mine are indeed 'complementary rather than contradictory', to quote an important essay by Tom Bartlett, developing one of Elliott's themes, that Tone's republicanism had important roots in the earlier 'Commonwealth' tradition. Critical in the ideology of the American revolutionary elite, this tradition, with its Renaissance and Enlightenment provenance, had *moral* views of 'civic virtue' and the 'popular will' at its core.

This brief rehearsal of recent historiography is not intended to be self-congratulatory (or, not only that!) but to make the point that there is little real controversy about Tone among historians. My attempt to understand him as a man of his time and class would appear provocative now mainly to some modern 'republicans', who claim to be his heirs, but have read little of his work, beyond the few hackneyed quotes wrenched out of context in the various short partisan 'selections' published this century. Like all of those, my own essay is long out of print, and it may be useful to outline briefly its argument about Tone's ideological development.[2]

Tone is best understood as a marginalised member of the Irish colonial ruling class. Despite his family's economic and social decline, he attracted sufficient patronage to be educated at Trinity College Dublin, but while he never lacked powerful friends, he failed to achieve a career commensurate with his expectations and undoubted talents. He made a half-hearted attempt to join the army in India, had a scheme to colonise the Sandwich Islands ignored by the British Government, didn't persevere at the Bar, and, despite some success as a propagandist, failed to attract sustained Whig patronage. Thus, over time, he became alienated from the ever-more reactionary and newly self-styled 'Ascendancy', and ultimately even from the imperial power, whose support alone made possible the Ascendancy's refusal to reform the system and open it to men of talent. While this made him a radical, and towards the end of his short life, a revolutionary separatist, his fundamental colonist perspectives changed little. His radicalism involved little more than a middle class take-over of the political system. Nationalism was a secondary and never well-developed part of his ideology. It was a by-product of his analysis of Ireland's unique colonial system, which initially led to the conclusion that only a union of the educated elites of Ireland's competing religions could undermine English support for Ascendancy power. Ultimately he came to believe that separation from England was a precondition for political reconstruction. What he called his 'new theory of politics' was little more than a particularly clear and coherent reformulation of the basic propositions of the Irish Whig tradition, which remained the most formative political influence of his life. He gave his 'new theory' its classic statement only in his last year, but at the same time claimed it as his political creed since the foundation of the United Irishmen. His 'objects' he then defined famously as 'To subvert the tyranny of our execrable government, to break the connection with England, the never-failing source of all our political evils, and to assert the independence of my country'. The 'means' emphasised were, 'to unite the whole people of Ireland ... to substitute the common name of Irishmen in place of the denominations of Protestant, Catholic and Dissenter'.[3]

This necessarily crude sketch of the ideological development of the remarkable young man, who celebrated a lonely thirty-third birthday in Paris in June 1796, four months after his arrival from America, brings into particular focus the combination of intense idealism and anxious careerism which characterised his journals, and is so well discussed by Elliott. What did his French experience add to that basic political position, beyond a hardening of its core propositions? Put another way, what aspects of contemporary France were particularly attractive to this experienced radical, as he developed, with remarkable rapidity and success, a political case which was both ideologically and pragmatically appealing to the French Government? While the Enlightenment idealisation of republican virtue is undoubtedly important in Tone's thought, most of his references to 'the Republic' were to the French version, as it had evolved by 1796. While this modified some of the key aspects of classical republicanism emphasised by Bartlett, it exaggerated others, especially its military basis. The growing militarism of this phase of the revolution appealed greatly to Tone on a number of levels, and it gave him a career that finally offered the role and fulfilment he had sought all his life. His Paris journals give a vivid picture of those aspects of French culture that interested him, particularly the theatre, and the theatricality of military display. What is almost entirely absent is any interest in revolutionary ideology, or the ferment of public debate, or even much reflection on the implications of French developments for Irish politics. As Elliott comments:

> Indeed what strikes one most about these journals ... of Tone's Paris mission is the infrequency of any mention of these concepts of nationhood, the armed struggle, or English tyranny.[4]

Tone's approval of the Directory's version of 'the Republic' came, above all, from a belief in strong government, a sufficient justification for its democratic deficiencies. Initially, he even wondered if it was powerful enough; a March 1796 journal entry welcomed a rumour that the Jacobins might return to power, 'for I think a little more energy just now would do the French government no harm'. The nervous gloss, 'not the terrorists, but the true original Jacobins who had begun the revolution', may be read as tacit acknowledgement that the 'terrorists' held some attraction.[5] The previous day's entry had explained that he had 'lied a little' when expressing reluctance to accept the French view that, after the success of the planned expedition, a military government would be necessary in Ireland,

> for my wishes are in favour of a very strong, or in other words, a military government at the outset, and if I had any share or influence on such a government, I think I would not abuse it, but I see

the handle it might give to demagogues if we had any such among us.[6]

The extent to which his French experiences brought out an authoritarian streak in Tone is best illustrated by his criticism of the Directory's mild treatment of the Royalist press, written shortly after the return of the Bantry expedition. While he would not wish to end press freedom, he wrote,

> I would almost certainly restrain it within just and reasonable limits ... In short I am of opinion, and if ever I have the opportunity I will endeavour to reduce that opinion to practice, that the government of a republic, properly organised, and freely and frequently chosen by the people, should be a strong government ... it is the people themselves who are insulted and degraded in the person of their government.[7]

The Jacobin identification of 'government' and 'people' in order to justify state repression is clearly echoed here.

This tendency was reinforced by the military ambience of his particular experience of France. Fascinated from boyhood by the colour and excitement of army life, his response to the offer of a commission in the French army was that it would be 'most honourable, and besides it is my passion'.[8] The future he hoped for in an independent Ireland was that of a professional soldier, and he almost certainly envisaged a similar role for an Irish army in the state as the French army then had.[9] It was not only 'the flower of the nation' but the nation itself.[10] 'It is in the armies that the Republic exists', he enthused, in one of his Bantry Bay entries.[11] This concept of 'the nation in arms' connects Tone's Jacobinism with the classical Republican idealism highlighted by Bartlett. His initial delight at being in France came in part from finding this familiar ideal a reality, and a model for Ireland. Two weeks after arriving, he wrote,

> In the evening walked to the Palais Royal, filled with the military ... I now perceive the full import of the expression, an armed nation, and I think I know a country that, for its extent and population could produce as many and as fine fellows as France.

Well, all in good time. It will be absolutely necessary to adopt measures similar to those which have raised and cherished this spirit here ... I think Ireland would be formidable as an armed nation.[12]

Writing six weeks later, he linked this ideal with fashionable notions of national character.

If we go to Ireland we must move heaven and earth to create the same spirit of enthusiasm which I see here, and from my observations of the Irish character, which so nearly resembles the French, I think it very possible. The devil of it is that poor Pat is a little given to drink and the French are very sober.[13]

Tone's journal reveals an engaging sense of fun, and he often included himself in the national weakness for excessive drinking. Making all allowance for humour, however, Tone reflected the typical colonist stereotype of 'the Irish properly so called', describing them also as 'very furious and savage', as well as improvident and easily led.[14] This view informed the scheme he proposed for recruiting Irish prisoners of war into the expeditionary forces, explaining, 'I know the Irish a little'. The prisoners should be brought to the port of embarkation, entertained with 'a large quantity of wine and brandy, a fiddle and some French *filles*, and then, when Pat's heart is a little soft', he could be talked into 'a trip once more to Ireland to see his people'.[15] That this was more than a joke is clear from his own account of how he recruited Irish prisoners eight months later, having plied them with drink and not telling them where they were going. They responded well because of 'the adventurous spirit of the nation'.[16]

A vital common element between men of all classes throughout Europe at this time was experience of army life, and enthusiasm for military culture. As Tone constantly pointed out to the French, the British army and navy depended heavily on Irish recruits, voluntary or otherwise. Together with the importance of the military in bringing colour and spectacle to daily life, even in remote areas, this fact accounts for the extent to which peasant secret societies mimicked army life in their organisation, rhetoric and rituals. The strong military ethos was also evident in ballads in English and poetry and songs in Irish. It would have provided an important basis for Tone in attempting to communicate with the local population, had the expedition landed. The centrality of military culture also provided a link with the century-old *Jacobite* tradition; French military help had long been a hope, though rarely a real expectation, and the tradition of the descendants of the old Gaelic elite serving in the army of France was well-known. On the other hand, the Jacobite military tradition was monarchical, Catholic and – more recently – anti-revolutionary, as was the Catholic hierarchy in their response to the threatened French invasion.

Initially thrilled to be 'an officer in the service of the French Republic', Tone soon had reason to worry about the implications.[17] Warned in July that the French envisaged 'direct interference' in any Irish government they helped to establish, then told it was proposed to send him with the expedition, he wrote,

> That stunned me a little. What could he mean? Am I to begin by representing the French Republic in Ireland, instead of representing the Irish Republic in France?[18]

From the beginning, he was acutely conscious of the imperialist dimension of French commitment to spreading their Revolution. In April 1796 he wrote in his journal, 'I for one will never be accessory to subjecting my counrty to the control of France, merely to get rid of that of England'.[19] He was perturbed particularly by the example of the French treatment of Holland and in July was denying to the French negotiator that Ireland could be treated similarly. The argument which he used was at odds with both democratic and nationalist principles, but it reflected a traditional Irish colonist position, that Ireland was not a conquered country.

> The French had conquered Holland, and had a right if they wished to throw it into the sea, but it was not so with Ireland. We rather resembled the situation of America in the last war.[20]

While he accepted that 'the French must have a very great influence on the measures of our government ... if they were wise they would not expect any direct interference'.[21] The same concern was articulated again on the eve of the expedition's departure,

> By what I see we have a little army of Commissaries who are going to Ireland to make their fortunes. If we arrive safe I think I will keep an eye a little on these gentlemen.[22]

Seven months after the disappointment at Bantry he was concerned at Napoleon's conduct in Italy as indicating 'the degree of influence which the French might have been disposed to arrogate to themselves in Ireland'.[23] Yet, his view on a proposed new expedition to Ireland a few weeks later was ambivalent. It was designed, he wrote,

> not merely to determine which of two despots shall sit upon a throne, or whether an island shall belong to this or that state; it is to change the destiny of Europe, to emancipate one, perhaps three nations; to open the sea to the commerce of the world; to found a new empire, to demolish an ancient one; to subvert a tyranny of six hundred years.[24]

This seems to imply that his stated aim, 'to subvert the tyranny of our execrable government, to break the connection with England' might well be achieved through absorption into the French empire. Certainly, in January 1798 he was busy justifying the French imposition of a new constitution and government on the Dutch, again citing the right of conquest and the failure of the Dutch to agree among themselves.

> I must once more acquit the French and I think that I should do so even in the case of my own country, if she were to show a similar incapacity in like circumstances, which, however, I am far from apprehending.[25]

That April he was rapturous at reports that Napoleon was planning an Egyptian campaign, even though this would mean the postponement of hopes of an attack on England. On the other hand, he was still seeking assurances about French intentions toward Ireland.

> ... the French Revolution is but yet begun; the Hercules is yet in swaddling bands. What a people! ... Once again I lose myself utterly in the contemplation of the present position of the Republic. What miserable pygmies we unfortunate Irish are! But that is no fault of ours; we may be better yet. It is a great consolation to me, the assurance of Merlin and Barras with regard to our independence – I count upon it firmly.[26]

In this and other journal entries there are hints of the spirit of adventure that had led Tone several times to propose a colonial scheme for the Sandwich Islands to the British government, and it seems clear that the longer Tone wore the French uniform, the more he saw himself as potentially in the service of the French empire as much as of the Republic. In May 1798 he offered his services for the rumoured expedition to India, 'notwithstanding that the age of enterprise is almost over with me ... It would be singular if, after all, I were to go to India. Twice or thrice already I have narrowly escaped the voyage'.[27] Three months later, he was instead on his way again to Ireland on what proved his final adventure. This is seen by Elliott as a gesture of despair after the collapse of the rebellion in Ireland and the weakening of his position in France.[28] At the end, his main concern was to insist on his rights as a French officer.

It remains a matter of speculation, therefore, how Tone might have represented the French revolution practically to 'the people of Ireland' had the expedition been successful. The way he represented the Irish situation to the French, while designed to encourage commitment to an expedition, also reflected the relative conservatism of his politics by late 1796. This is particularly true of his views on 'the Irish properly so called', his revealing description of the 'peasantry of Ireland'.[29] No phrase in Tone's journal has been more taken out of context than that indicating sympathy with 'the men of no property'. He used it once only, after an account of a discussion in March 1796 with the French government representative Delacroix, who had discouraged expectations of a large expedition, such as Tone had argued would attract 'those men of property whose assistance was so essential in framing a government in Ireland'. The context makes it clear that it was simply as part of the attempt to win over the French that Tone was prepared to argue,

> If the men of property will not support us they must fall; we can support ourselves by the aid of that numerous and respectable class of the community, the men of no property.[30]

He continued to believe, and to argue, however, that the men of property would lead the coming Irish revolution, as they had those of America and France.[31] Indeed throughout his writings Tone showed remarkably little interest in, or understanding of, the problems of the Irish poor, although these had been highlighted by agrarian insurgency for over thirty years. On social, as on most political issues, Tone was markedly more conservative than other United Irish leaders of similar background.[32]

Tone was, however, well-informed on one particular aspect of peasant insurgency, the rapid politicisation of the Catholic secret society, the Defenders, through the absorption of French ideas and the development of French contacts. In his Irish journals Tone had been concerned that the middle class Catholic Committee should quieten the agitation, but in his key 'Memorials' on the state of Ireland for the French in February 1796, he was keen to emphasise Defender strength.[33]

> The fact is that in June last it embraced the whole peasantry of the provinces of Ulster, Leinster and Connaught in three-fourths of the nation; and I have little doubt but it has since extended into Munster ... These men who are called Defenders are completely organised on a military plan, divided according to their respective districts and officered by men chosen by themselves ... and whose object is the emancipation of their country, the subversion of English usurpation and the bettering the condition of the wretched peasantry of Ireland. The eyes of this whole body ... are turned with the most anxious expectation to France for assistance and support.[34]

The French, however, persisted in seeing the Irish poor more in terms of the Catholic peasants of the Vendée, priest-led and bitter foes of the revolution. Hoche asked Tone, 'Was there no danger of the Catholics setting up one of their own chiefs for king?'[35] and all his French contacts worried about the role of the priests, unimpressed by Tone's breezy predictions of the speedy demise of Catholicism in Ireland once the French had prevailed. Likewise, when Hoche asked:

> Who were the Orange boys? I explained it to him, adding that, as to them, it was an affair of no consequence which we would settle in three days on our arrival.[36]

Tone's 'Address to the peasantry of Ireland', while it rehearsed 'the great benefits which the revolution had procured for the peasants of France', had few echoes of the grievances long expressed by agrarian secret societies and did not indicate an easy rapport with the local population, had the French landed.[37]

Tone continued to keep his journal during the frustrating wait in Bantry Bay, and it conveys better than any other source the combined concerns about the weather, and the fear of being trapped by the English fleet which led to the abrupt decision on 26 December 'to cut our cable and put to sea instantly'. The few passages that give an insight into wider and more political concerns are at odds with the traditional view of Tone, but they confirm the picture given by his journal over the previous year. On 23 December he wrote:

> I am now so near the shore that I can in a manner touch the sides of Bantry Bay with my right and left hand, yet God knows whether I shall ever tread again on Irish ground. There is one thing which I am surprised at, which is the extreme *sang-froid* with which I view the coast. I expected I should have been violently affected; yet I look at it as if it were the coast of Japan. I do not, however, love my country the less for not having romantic feelings with regard to her.[38]

Leaving aside the fact that – on a variety of levels – West Cork was indeed for Tone a foreign and exotic country, this is a reminder that his nationalism, like his republicanism, had an older Enlightenment and Whig basis and bore little relationship to most shades of Irish republicanism which later claimed him as their founder. This is further evident in what he wrote as the reduced fleet left Bantry on 26 December,

> Well, England has not had such an escape since the Spanish Armada ... Well, let me think no more about it; it is lost and let it go! I am now a Frenchman and must regulate my future plans accordingly. I hope the Directory will not dismiss me the Service for this unhappy failure, in which certainly I have nothing personally to reproach myself with ... I am as eager to get back to France as I was to come to Ireland.[39]

During the remainder of his short life, as we have seen, he was to conflate service to 'the Republic' with service to the empire which Napoleon was busy creating.

THE SOUTH MUNSTER REGION IN THE 1790s

DAVID DICKSON

Desolate and remote as it may have seemed from ship-board in December 1796, Bantry Bay lay within a region that had witnessed remarkable economic and social changes in the lifetime of its oldest inhabitants. It was part of an integrated commercial zone which we may label South Munster. This in turn had been created by the rise of a new international centre of Atlantic trade – Cork city, the economic tentacles of which had crossed old cultural boundaries and bound together west Waterford and Co. Cork with central and south Kerry – roughly from Dungarvan to Tralee. Land prices and farming patterns, diet and drink, clothing and housing, all had been profoundly affected by the intensity of commercialisation within the force-field of Cork. Indeed by the standards of the late eighteenth-century Atlantic world, the city on the marsh was a relative giant: in the autumn cattle-slaughtering season there were probably as many as 60,000 human sardines squeezed into what is now the core of the modern city.

The region, the wholesale catchment area of Cork city, was of course a heterogeneous one in terms of natural endowment, with huge east/west contrasts in soil quality and grazing capacity. But it had important common denominators: the climate was, is, mild by Irish standards, and early grass and early harvests gave its farmers valuable relative advantage. In addition there was the exceptionally high percentage of tilled land close to the sea and to the many navigable rivers. The intensely peninsularised character of the south-west, and the Bandon, east Bride and Blackwater river systems allowed the large-scale use of shore-based resources (sand and seaweed for fertiliser) and offered cheap bulk transport to urban markets. Furthermore, South Munster had been exposed to the rise of the North Atlantic trading systems of Great Britain, Holland and

France since the 1650s, and was better placed in relation to inter-continental shipping and convoy routes than any other comparable Irish region. Strong albeit unstable overseas demand for salted beef and butter, hides, pork, tallow and barley had continued to grow for more than a century, and the monetisation of social relations continued as a slow but inexorable process, an evolution mediated through a variety of local players – city merchants and local shippers, entrepreneurial landlords and the master-dairymen who leased out cows in small herds to those too poor to possess their own.

In two further respects the region stood out: by the 1790s it was very well populated by Irish standards, having witnessed stronger demographic growth over a longer span than most other regions – the population around Bantry Bay was probably four times more numerous than it had been when last a French fleet had dropped anchor there in 1689. Abundant cheap labour was the vital under-pinning of a vibrant capitalistic agrarian system. South Munster was also a zone that by general Irish standards had been powerfully affected, for ill or good, by seventeenth-century English immigration and eighteenth-century Protestant social engineering on the part of gentry, clergy and a state apparatus that remained profoundly anti-Catholic. This combination of economic prosperity and ethno-religious tension is reflected in much of the abundant contemporary Gaelic poetry of the region, unpublished then but already widely diffused. Outside observers tended only to see transformed landscapes and material cultures in transition. Charles Vallancey, military engineer, antiquarian and regular visitor to the region contrasted the west Cork of the early 1760s, when 'it was so thinly inhabited' that 'an army of 10,000 men could not possibly have found subsistence between Bantry and Bandon' with the situation twenty years later: 'the sides of the hills are under the plough, the verges of the bogs are reclaimed and the southern coast from Skibereen to Bandon is one continued garden of grain and potatoes ...'.[1] Other less adventurous visitors praised the man-made beauty of Cork Harbour, studded with merchant villas and gentry 'seats', or the reforestation of the Blackwater valley as newly planted hardwoods marked out the succession of classical 'big houses' from Millstreet to Youghal; by the 1790s there were about 500 such houses and demesnes in South Munster.

One can distinguish three types of rural community that had evolved across the region. First, there were the districts of social complexity where rural society below the landowners had several distinct tiers of status and wealth, notably a cattle-owning and comfortable farming stratum and, one or two rungs below, a near-landless class primarily dependent on local farmers giving their menfolk casual employment; tillage production was highly important in such districts, which tended to be in the north and east of the region. Second were the districts of social homogeneity but occupational complexity – where farming, fishing and rural industry were interlocked: this was the pattern in much of south-west Cork and on the Dingle peninsula. Then there were the many districts which had very few gentry and both social and occupational homogeneity; these were the parishes where pastoral farming remained the principal livelihood – upland and inaccessible areas out of which seasonal migration was often necessary to make the rent, the tithe, the hearth tax and the spending money for the fair.

How would these landscapes of 200 years ago compare with a seagull's-eye view today? The total human population of South Munster in the 1790s was not much different from the 1990s levels, the 1790s total being probably somewhat higher, but the striking visual difference was that the 1790s population was far more rural, more dispersed and, despite coastal clustering in the south-west, better camouflaged thanks to the predominance of organic roofing materials. Yet every thatch or sod-roofed house had its garden, not of flowers but of potatoes and cabbages; nearly every rural household had at least the proverbial acre, and thus most families supplied most of their food needs domestically – in complete contrast to the pattern of the 1990s. Farmland across most of the region was enclosed in rough fields, but in most districts these were far smaller than modern divisions. The seagull of the 1790s would have seen very little woodland or forest, certainly none of the insidious swathes of conifer of the 1990s. The wild native hardwoods had been cleared by the 1750s from virtually everywhere except around the Killarney lakes, and the gentry's decorative woodlands were still young, although proliferating in the favoured districts. On the hills, as Vallancey implied, a soaring spade culture was reaching altitudes higher than are now being farmed, much higher than even the coarse grazing limits in many parishes until EU sheep schemes temporarily reversed things. The process of bogland and upland reclamation had another forty years to run in many inland districts – in Sliabh Luachra for example – but settlement along the south-west coast was reaching saturation point before 1800.

Across the rural sky-line, apart from the big houses and the equally ubiquitous abandoned castles, stood dozens of churches, the more visible and substantial of which were those of the Church of Ireland – a striking profusion in the Bandon valley reflecting the local density of rural Protestant settlement. Catholic worship was certainly public in the 1790s, but still located largely under thatch and in unpretentious barn-like structures.

Our proverbial bird would see few secondary roads, a very limited number of bridges, and not much wheeled traffic away from the arterial roads. The small urban settlement of Bantry had two roads by 1796, but neither guaranteed an easy passage for wheeled traffic in wet seasons. The countryside was however alive with garranes (the small working horses), petty sailing vessels, and folk on the move by foot along the myriad of tracks and rights of way that criss-crossed every parish. Sea links were the critical means of communication for wholesale trade, and thus there were uncounted thousands of mainly timber vessels at work between Ring and Fenit employed at different tasks in different seasons, agricultural, piscatorial and commercial. All, or almost all of the carriage-roads led to Cork, which was probably five times the size of the second town in the region, Bandon. The city had broken out of its island site in the seventeenth century, and had witnessed the demolition of the last of its old walls at the beginning of the eighteenth. Its fate was in the hands of the one to two hundred wholesale merchants, many of whom were also dabbling in water-powered industry, urban development and rural property speculation. They shared many cultural tastes, including a liking for ornate suburban retreats, but were divided as to religious affiliation. In actual numbers Catholic wholesaling firms were in a majority, but Protestant capital and Protestant conspicuous consumption were more in evidence.

So much for the visible. What of the patterns of power and their locus? By nineteenth-century standards, the hand of the state was still weak, but it was becoming perceptibly stronger: where once, thirty or forty years previously, a smuggling-based black economy had flourished along the south-west peninsulas and in Iveragh, the effectiveness of the revenue service was now being felt, sometimes violently so, in the 1780s and 1790s. An improved postal service helped the magistracy (i.e., those resident gentry and clergy well enough regarded by their peers and superiors to be appointed to the commission of the peace) provide the beginnings of a real intelligence system for Dublin Castle by 1798. In explicitly military terms, the Volunteer movement in the previous decade had been the last great display of local proprietorial independence against the state; the militia (created in 1793), the yeomanry (in 1796) and even the regular army offered much scope for the operation of local patronage, but to varying degrees all these forces were circumscribed by state-wide regulatory and command structures.

Gentry power, so formidable in rural society for much of the eighteenth century, was being diminished. But of course gentry influence, inasmuch as it mediated the superior power of the state, was unevenly balanced: rival regional alliances struggled for the lion's share of government patronage, and in South Munster the lion had usually been successive heads of the Boyles of Castlemartyr, ennobled with the earldom of Shannon in 1756. The second earl (1727–1807) enjoyed an uncertain ascendancy; it was based on the traditional family ingredients of conservative ideology, prudent parliamentary gamesmanship and the cultivation of a menagerie of regional clients, cousins and dependants. Shannon was challenged by

89

other landed coalitions (for a time the most formidable included the Longfields, Kings and Whites of Bantry), but two more permanent alternative centres of regional power were emerging: Cork city business (excluding of course the conservative friends of the Shannon interest but including a number of wealthy Catholic traders) formed one such alternative; the Hely Hutchinsons, earls of Donoughmore, were this group's political mouth-piece. The Catholic hierarchy led by Bishops Moylan and Coppinger, and the vestigial Catholic landed interest led by Viscount Kenmare, were another; however the political influence of this group was essentially covert in the 1790s and insofar as it registered in Dublin Castle it was as a result of direct contact and lobbying, not through the mobilising of local public opinion.

WHAT CONNECTION WAS THERE BETWEEN these developments within the region and the expatriate project that led to Bantry Bay? Very little might seem the answer if we are to take at face value the famous jibe of poet and United Irishman Micheál Óg Ó Longáin against his neighbours: 'Where are the Munstermen, or is it true they still are alive?'[2] There was no supportive *jacquerie* when news of the French fleet was broadcast around the region. And in 1797–8 the second city of the kingdom presented no security threat remotely comparable to that posed by Dublin or Belfast. Was the 'affray' near Clonakilty in June '98 the gravest challenge that 'rebel Cork' could offer the political establishment at its gravest hour?[3]

The relative tranquillity of the Cork region despite expectations to the contrary is a fascinating problem. One line of argument would emphasise fortuitous contingency: that the region was perceived by government to be a soft target for French attack and was therefore assigned an exceptionally strong garrison on the ground, with the result that revolutionary activity was suffocated. Certainly it was seen to be a troubled and troublesome area: the economic difficulties of the decade had hit the region particularly hard – inflation, some very poor harvests, and the near paralysis of conventional maritime trade as the war with France intensified. The rising tide was no longer lifting all South Munster boats: the vulnerable and the insecure were becoming more numerous and more distressed; side by side, or rather above them, a wealthier yet politically disadvantaged Catholic strong farmer/trader stratum had become a more conspicuous feature in the social landscape. The collapse in the incomes of cereal farmers in the autumn of 1797 affected parts of South Munster as severely as it did Co. Wexford, and the apocalyptic fears of some magistrates during the winter of 1797 that rural rebellion was in the offing reinforced the strategic decision of Dublin Castle to saturate South Munster with militia forces; huge numbers were concentrated at the camp beside Bandon. This official perception, both of Cork's combustibility and its vulnerability, led to a campaign of pre-emptive disarming of many parishes from Carbery in the west to Imokilly in the east during April and May 1798. Had it not been for the supposedly firm but temperate actions of Generals Stewart ·and Moore, Cork would have been a second Wexford – that was the judgement of some gentry observers.

Another explanation for the region's quiescence was that the United Irish organisation in the Cork region had failed to develop the critical mass required to prepare for a serious military challenge. And there had been no constitutional United Irish society in Cork in 1791–2 (even Limerick and Clonmel briefly had such clubs). The prior history of parliamentary electioneering in both Cork city and county may have had something to do with this; competition between the leading gentry candidates at the general elections of 1783 and 1790 had been intense, but no faction espousing Catholic relief or advanced reform had emerged to challenge the main contestants. Even in the city the Catholic group connected with the Hely Hutchinsons was an essentially conservative lobby.

A further barrier to radical politics in the city was the weakness of craft politics: thanks to the peculiar evolution of the civic constitution of Cork, trade guilds had not come to occupy the crucial electoral role that they did in Dublin, and this profoundly affected local political culture. In Dublin the guilds had been the training grounds for craftsmen-politicians and for street radicals, whereas Cork's municipal government since the 1740s had been controlled by the 'Friendly Club', a large but closed group of several hundred freemen; thus the trade guilds had lacked a political role. This fact plus the more precarious demographic position of the Protestant artisans compared to their Dublin brothers made the task of the home-grown radicals in Cork a far more daunting one.[4]

Yet a number of Cork men did emerge to play centre-stage in radical and revolutionary politics at the national level – in Dublin and beyond – Arthur O'Connor, the Sheares brothers, John Daly Burk, and Richard Dry being the most prominent. Attendance at Trinity College by a number of the Cork activists may have provided the opportunity for crucial friendships to be made as well as for political education; 15 per cent of those entering the college in the early 1790s were Cork-born; 5 of the 19 expelled in April 1798 for suspected United Irishmen links were from South Munster.

Government informers, like the barrister Leonard Mc-Nally, began to paint a picture of Cork city as a hot-bed of dis-affected revolutionaries by 1795, and Burk himself, writing some years later, claimed that the Sheares brothers had estab-lished a Jacobin club in the city around that time.[5] This may have been connected to Henry Sheares's decision to contest the by-election for one of the city seats in 1795: his opponent, Richard Hare, was son of probably the wealthiest Protestant merchant of his generation and was soon to be ennobled as Baron Ennismore. Hare received 308 votes, Sheares 18.

More telling evidence of local support for democratic prin-ciples and friendship with France was the survival and relative success of the *Cork Gazette*, run by Denis Driscol. His intellect-ual odyssey from Catholic seminarian to radical deist earned him prison for seditious libel and eventual American exile, but not before he had managed to publish, albeit erratically, a newspaper for some six years; even by Belfast standards it adopted extreme positions on social reform and religious speculation, to the fascination if not the edification of its read-ers.[6]

The *Gazette* folded in the autumn of 1797 at the threat of

another prosecution of its editor; by that stage large-scale subversive organisation in and around Cork city was at last under way. Several factors contributed to this: the intensity of the regional economic crisis in the course of 1797; the circulation of various 'emissaries' from Dublin, most of whom had strong local connections, who were seeking to build up the oathbound cellular 'Union'; the bitter fall-out from the summer general election in the city in which large numbers of newly enfranchised Catholic freeholders had taken part. The contest had for the first time had an ostensibly sectarian dimension, and a new fear of the Orangemen – real or imagined, local or far distant – seems to have crept into popular Catholic consciousness very quickly, notably in the city and in west Cork.[7]

It is not yet apparent which stimuli were most potent in broadening United Irish support in South Munster between mid-1797 and May 1798. It is clear however that great numbers were sworn as United Irishmen in the old city suburbs (notably Blackpool and Blarney Lane), the Liberties, in parishes eastwards through Imokilly and around Youghal, in Roche's Country along the rich valleys of the middle Blackwater and its tributaries, reaching far into west Waterford. Another area successfully penetrated was the Bandon valley. A characteristic common to most of these areas was that their social structure was complex and stratified, their agriculture heavily biased towards tillage, and comfortable farmers were in economic control of local destinies.

The woollen draper John Swiney, one of the key city organisers and later a state prisoner, made extravagant claims after the event as to the numbers sworn for the city and county of Cork (16,000 and 60,000 respectively), with 4,000 organised for collective action in the city.[8] Passive support was apparently not a problem for United Irish organisers nor indeed does there seem to have been any question as to the ability of local cells at parish level to organise themselves; the weakness was rather in the chain of command between the city and the rural world outside.

This can be seen interpreted in two lights: possibly there was a failure on the part of those at county level and above to give strategic leadership and direction to the Munster revolutionary movement, a reflection perhaps on the competence of the Sheares brothers whose role in specifically South Munster matters remains elusive. Certainly the arrest of the Sheares brothers on the eve of the Leinster rebellion was said to have thrown the Cork men into confusion. But another reading of the feebleness of revolutionary organisation in Munster may touch on a deeper issue: whether or not there was a cultural gap between the literate, largely anglophone enthusiasts for democracy and 'the brotherhood of affection' in the city, and the largely Irish-speaking countrymen of the hinterland whose consumption of the new print culture was limited and whose motivation to rise with 'the children of the Gael' was merely reactive and backward-looking.

This must remain speculative. The impact of the new politics on the comfortable farming classes should not be underestimated, but the fact remains that the regional legacy of '98, at least for those who lived through 'the radical moment', was one of heightened sectarianism and religious polarisation, albeit in the context of permanently widened political horizons.

BANTRY BAY – THE WIDER CONTEXT

KEVIN WHELAN

In December 1797, the following United Irishman catechism was reported from the Cloyne area of County Cork. Pointing 'to a switch or whip,' the recruiter initiated a sequence of set questions and answers by asking:

What is that in your hand?	It is a branch.
Of what?	Of the Tree of Liberty
Where did it first grow?	In America.
Where does it bloom?	In France.
Where did the seeds fall?	In Ireland.
When will the moon be full?	When the four quarters meet.

The correspondent glossed the last answer as referring to 'that imminent period' when 'the four provinces meet in rebellion'.[1] The circulation of this catechism in east Cork demonstrates that the United Irishmen were establishing themselves in the rich tillage lands of Imokilly: the sequencing shows a strong sense of the 'Atlantic Revolution' of the last quarter of the eighteenth century which the radicals wished to introduce into Ireland; its final question demonstrates awareness of the need to build the organisation to the appropriate level of national cohesion before launching their revolutionary strike. The French fleet at Bantry Bay fitted into these three sets of scenarios – international, national and local.

While the catechism (and historians) have tended to stress the wholesale importation of revolutionary ideology, it is crucial not to lose sight of the indigenous roots of radicalism, nor the extent to which second-hand sedition from America and France impacted on a well-developed existing political culture. Eighteenth-century Munster, especially the fertile valleys within reach of Cork city, had witnessed intense economic growth, based around commercial farming, in-

95

cluding dairying, tillage and cattle fattening. The resultant tremendous prosperity was achieved only at the expense of the advanced proletarianisation of the agricultural labour force, widely seen as among the most immiserated social groups in Europe and increasingly dependent on a monotonous potato diet as the century reached its conclusion. The 1740–41 famine, long remembered as 'Bliain an Áir' had taken a horrific toll on the Munster poor: one observer wrote of the people 'eating grass like a beast,' of 'the helpless orphan exposed on the dunghill and none to take him in for fear of infection,' and of 'the hungry infant sucking at the breast of the already expired parent.'[2] By 1787, the Attorney-General could declare that 'it was impossible for the peasantry of Munster any longer to exist in the extreme wretchedness under which they laboured. A poor man was to pay £6 for an acre of potato ground, which £6 he was obliged to work out with his landlord at 5d. per day' [288 days work].[3] In 1796, the Corkman John Philpot Curran claimed that the corn laws had the effect of 'more than doubling the price of land, of more than doubling the price of every article of necessary consumption, without proportionately increasing the wages of the labourer.'[4]

These volatile conditions of unexampled prosperity and cheek-by-jowl poverty were incubators of agrarian stress. Munster was the cockpit of the redresser secret societies, the Whiteboys and the Rightboys. The Whiteboys originated in the 1760s, their initial stimulus being the privatisation of hitherto communal hill pastures. Within the traditional agrarian system, no rights were more sacrosanct or zealously defended than these communal rights on open grazing ground. The Munster Whiteboys declared:

> We, levellers and avengers for the wrongs done to the poor, have unanimously assembled to raze walls and ditches that have been made to inclose the commons. Gentlemen now of late have learned to grind the face of the poor so that it is impossible for them to live. They cannot even keep a pig or a hen at their doors. We warn them not to raise again either walls or ditches in the place of those we destroy, nor even to inquire about the destroyers of them. If they do, their cattle shall be houghed and their sheep

laid open in the fields.[5]

In the expansive conditions, the small farmers and labourers were being squeezed, as described from the Mallow district in 1775:

> The country about Mallow and I believe all over Munster is of late years much thinned and stripped of its inhabitants to make room for bullocks, sheep and dairy cows. Rich folks were never half so fond as they have been within these 10 or 12 years past of taking farms and increasing their stocks of cattle.[6]

The Whiteboy dynamic emerged out of this conflict between the moral economy (with its egalitarian ethos) and the immoral economy (with its commercial orientation). Munster simmered through the last half of the eighteenth century, with occasional eruptions into large-scale disturbances. In 1775, a defender of the Whiteboys offered five defences of their existence: (1) The Whiteboys were part of a general European pattern 'occasioned by the tyranny and oppression of the great and rich.' (2) 'The small farmers and cottiers of Ireland were as wretched slaves as any upon the face of the earth.' (3) 'Their food, apparel and squalid cabins make hanging or any other kind of death more desirable than life.' (4) 'That though they live in a rich and fertile country, all their industry is inadequate to a rate of thirty shillings for a rood of potato ground, additionally charged with a crown or three shillings for the tythe of it.' (5) 'That honest old improving tenants are cast off every day by mercenary landlords, to make room for a higher bidder by six pence an acre.' If such leases were renewed to the existing tenants, it would 'lower the exorbitant price of lands' and enable the tenants 'to deal charitably with their cottiers.'[7]

To this oppositional agrarian tradition was added the existence of a well-developed Jacobitism in Munster. The counties of Tipperary, Cork and Clare had the highest rate of 'Wild Geese' recruitment, while their Catholic 'underground gentry' retained close links with the Jacobite officer corps in Continental armies.[8] This Catholic interest was especially strong in the Blackwater Valley, among families like the Cotters, Nagles and Hennessys. The Munster Gaelic poets lauded the Stuarts in their verse, and the aisling (allegory) genre was pre-eminently a Munster speciality. The existence of this Jacobite strain was crucial in inhibiting the development of a fully-formed Hanoverian loyalty among Munster Catholics, creating a vacuum which other forms of politics could easily fill. Balancing Catholic Jacobitism was an equally entrenched Francophobic and partisan Protestant interest among the Munster gentry, notably in leading 'political' families like the Boyles, Maudes, Beresfords and Musgraves. Four of the sectarian flashpoints of eighteenth-century Ireland – the Cotter, O'Sullivan, Sheehy and O'Leary episodes – occurred in Munster. It was also Munster, in the form of Bishop Woodward, who initiated the strident 'paper war' of the 1780s, which culminated in the clarification of the concept of 'Protestant ascendancy.' This highly charged Munster milieu also generated some of the most independent and challenging minds of the period – including Edmund Burke, James Barry, John Daly Burk, John Philpot Curran and Daniel O'Connell.

The American and French Revolutions therefore impacted on an existing polarisation: they did not initiate *de novo* a new politics. A Cork poet, Colman MacCartaigh, reacted to the American Revolution by fusing the new developments with the older Jacobite tradition and his own personal situation. Having reviewed progress in America by extolling the exploits of Washington, Jones and Lee, and having assessed the European implications of the war, MacCartaigh then shifted his focus to the Irish situation. He commented on the Volunteer arrays at Dungannon and Ballinasloe and how they were overawing a cowed London, predicting that a free trade would be speedily granted. The poem then reverts to the Jacobite mode: Charles will regain his kingdoms, the Catholic religion will be restored to its proper dignity and the indigenous Irish will regain their usurped role at the head of society. There is one final twist in the poem's tail. MacCartaigh launches a searing rant against the English settlers (Saxons) in Ireland. It is difficult not to see here an insistent millenarian impulse, with its emphasis on role reversal and rapid change, but the power of the verse issues from its densely observed account of the condition of the poet and its displacement onto the new order after a successful Jacobite restoration:

Here are the Things I Wish for the Saxons
Vomiting and Diarrhoea, Shivers and Shakes and Heartaches
A Cold Cabin Blinded With Smoke
The Rain Dripping Down on Them From Monday to Saturday
A Hard Floor, As a Bed, With a Scatter of Straw
Fleas and Lice Constantly at Them

Thrashing, Binding, and Hoeing
Turning the Sod and Burning the Lime
Digging the Drains and Making Ditches

Their Best Meal White Bucks [bad potatoes]
With No Dip Only a Grain of Salt
Scalding Porridge That Will Give Them Indigestion
And May Anyone That Gives Them More Get A Heart Attack.[9]

This aggressive millenarianism, this unstable mix of old and new, this grafting of personal circumstances onto the political process, this expectation of the reversal of history were characteristics shared by the Catholic poor of both Munster and South Ulster – the two most structurally impoverished and marginalised groups in Irish society. Both developed an oppositional stance, reflected in the Whiteboy and Defender movements. It is also suggestive that both areas had the strongest survival of the Gaelic literary tradition.

The seeming mimicry by Ireland of the American trajectory towards independence from the imperial centre quickly became distorted in the mid 1780s, when the parliamentary reform movement split acrimoniously over the issue of admitting Catholics to full participation in the hitherto exclusively Protestant polity. The impact of the French Revolution was to free up this sterile sectarian stalemate: as Tone's famous *Argument* cogently demonstrated, if French Catholics could display such obvious political maturity, then so too could their Irish counterparts. Catholics could be admitted to the Irish polity without reservation and the United Irishmen were founded simultaneously in Belfast and Dublin in 1791 to give cohesion and momentum to this innovation in Irish politics. The resulting alliance of advanced reformers, notably the Belfast Presbyterians and the independent Dublin interest, with Catholic activists signalled a startling rupture with the British Whig tradition and the Scottish Enlightenment. The United Irishmen broke with the sedimented anti-popery of the Whigs; unlike the Scots, they pursued a separatist rather than integrationist agenda; uniquely within the European Enlightenment, they developed a novel approach which conferred parity of esteem on regional cultures (unlike the dominant strand of Enlightenment thought, especially in the Scottish and French variants, which consigned them to inevitable erasure under the name of rational progress). The Belfast Harp Festival of 1792, and the Irish-language miscellany *Bolg an Tsolair* of 1795 were the most obvious public expressions of this remarkable development.

The French Revolution had one other pronounced effect in Ireland: it appreciably quickened the pulse of political change. As Hegel argued, ancient time was now terminated and history had rejuvenated itself in a new cycle of progress. 'The great metaphors of renewal, of the creation by a second coming of secular grace of a just rational city for man, took on the urgent drama of concrete possibility. The eternal tomorrow of utopian political vision became, as it were, Monday morning.'[10] Radicalism acquired a buoyant vehemence: even the preternaturally cautious Catholic leaders of Ireland, hitherto demurely patient at the glacially slow thaw in Protestant attitudes, were affected. Previously ideologically invertebrate, they now acquired a stiff spine which, for the first time, allowed them to survey the political landscape from above the parapet of the Penal Laws, held in suspended animation over them for a century. Bishop Hussey pinpointed the change in 1790:

> One cannot foresee what a continuation of oppressive laws may work upon the minds of the people; and those of the Irish Catholics are much altered within my own memory and they will not in future bear the lash of tyranny and oppression which I have seen inflicted upon them, without their resisting or even complaining.[11]

As the United Irishmen set about politicising the masses, colonial chickens fluttered back to their sectarian perches. In an astute commentary, the well informed George Knox analysed the situation in 1793, pinpointing the absence of hegemony as the fatal flaw in Irish society, and assigning its frailty to the oppressive legacy of Irish history:

> It is the misfortune of Ireland that the rich & poor form two such distinct bodies, having different language, habits, religion & objects, the consequence of the colonising system. The whole country has not grown up together as in England where a sort of relationship subsists amongst all classes of the people. There the rich & the poor are separated from each other by such a gradation that they can neither of them be addressed & worked upon as a body. Here, there is a strong line drawn between them & they feel that their interests are distinct. The only influence of the rich is from the servility and timidity of the poor but he has none from attachment or feudal feelings. The consequence is that any cunning low man can win the peasant from his landlord with the greatest ease & in times of public commotion will certainly do so.[12]

These considerations had intensified force once France and Britain went to war in 1793. The ensuing titanic struggle was the first modern war, an ideological war (as opposed to earlier contests fought merely for strategic or dynastic advantage) between republicanism and monarchy, between democracy and the Ancien Régime. The war had practical repercussions in Ireland. The United Irishmen, barely tolerated in peacetime, were ruthlessly suppressed as potential traitors in wartime. Strategic consideration ensured that Ireland could be an invasion target, an invitingly soft underbelly for a treacherous French strike. The south-west, especially Cork Harbour, was always judged to be the most likely landing spot, as it was closest to France, had friendly prevailing winds, and possessed the alluring magnet of Cork city, one of the premier provision ports of the Atlantic world. The fortification of Cork Harbour and its saturation with troops proceeded in the 1790s, in response to the French threat.

In the wake of their suppression, the United Irishmen

faced an agonising choice. Should they tamely acquiesce in their suppression, and await a more propitious political climate or should they instead seize the proffered gauntlet, and develop a revolutionary organisation capable of seizing that power which it was now blatantly obvious would never be ceded to them by a corrupt political process? This choice chafed at an existing tension within the movement between an 'Enlightenment' (Drennan, Butler, Rowan) and 'social radical' (Neilson, Russell, Tone) tendency.[13] The mainly Belfast-based radical group argued that their highly successful paper war had now to be supplemented by a preparation for a military contest. From their Belfast base, this group began in 1794 to reorganise the earlier 'open' societies into an 'affiliated' system of 35-member cells, basically comprising the hard-core of old Volunteer companies, which had never entirely disintegrated in east Ulster. By mid 1795, seventy-five 'simple' societies existed within a twenty mile radius of Belfast, plus county organisations in Antrim and Down, and an embryonic Ulster directory comprised of well-known figures. Samuel Neilson in particular created this disciplined cellular base, welded onto a sophisticated hierarchical command structure, based on the barony, county and province. Each three cells amalgamated into a parish-based company of 100 men, commanded by a captain: each company was broken into ten townland-based platoons, commanded by a sergeant. Ten companies created a baronial-based regiment, commanded by a colonel. The county army was composed of these regiments, commanded by an adjutant general elected by the colonels. In this way, the United Irishmen sought to retain the principle of horizontal democratic representation within a hierarchical system of centralised control.

The celebrated Cave Hill meeting in June 1795 consolidated the new departure. It was agreed to transfer the affiliated system to Dublin, even in the face of protracted opposition. Tighter links would be forged between Dublin and Belfast and between the United Irishmen and the Catholic radicals (newly receptive to their overtures after the Fitzwilliam debacle). Three other gambits were also agreed: to merge the Defenders into the expanding United Irish network (thereby giving them control over mid and south Ulster), to infiltrate the army and militia, and to despatch Tone to France as a fully briefed and accredited ambassador.

The process of transferring the 'affiliated' or Ulster system to a divided Dublin society was painfully slow. The old leadership resisted and only finally relinquished control in September 1796.[14] In the interim, the seeds of the new system had been laid by 'Citizen' Burk among the radical Dublin proletariat, especially in the Liberties. The new departure, opening out to the Defenders and the Dublin poor, required a toughening of the United Irishmen's social radical stance. Rather than deliberately avoiding, as before, the glaring inequalities of Irish life, the United Irishmen now tried to face them, and in understanding them, had recourse to the divisive colonial past. This turn towards a materialist and historically-grounded critique of the Irish problem had an immense populist appeal. It is at this stage, for example, that Denis Taaffe and Watty Cox, two of their most aggressive, acerbic and pungent polemicists, joined the movement. Sympathy for the poor now becomes a prominent part of United Irish thinking. Tone observed: 'God help the poor for they are able to help nobody and therefore nobody cares for them.'[15]

By systematically offering political participation and the rights of citizenship to the 'men of no property', the United Irishmen raised the stakes in the battle for minds and hearts. The old grievances of the poor, hitherto addressed directly only by the agrarian secret societies – tithes, taxes, rents, living conditions – were now linked for the first time to a significant national organisation, with a well-defined programme for radical reform. The United Irishmen developed a striking ability to translate abstract principles into issues of real meaning out of doors, especially the gifted populists, Burk, Cox and Taaffe, and witty pamphleteers like William Sampson and Thomas Russell. The *Northern Star* acquired a sharper edge, accentuated in its successor *The Press* and audaciously present in the abrasive *Union Star*. These developments were aided by the United Irishmen's access to quality printing: their newspapers, while kept cheap, were technically advanced and had coherent and sophisticated distribution networks.

This populist tinge and aggressive stance did not appeal to the more cerebral figures in the movement; Drennan judged these products to be 'vulgar for the vulgar,' as opposed to his own Ciceronian confections. His disdain exposed the sharpness of the divide within the United Irishmen over attitudes to the poor, especially the Catholic poor. The Drennan wing continued to despise the poor as 'the swinish multitude,' incapable of understanding or exercising political rights: they differed from Burke only in explaining their squalid condition as the diseased product of gothic government, which could only be ameliorated by a lengthy educational and political rehabilitation. In their contaminated state, the poor presented a lethal threat to United Irish principles and it was irresponsible to seek to involve them in a revolutionary organisation. Their brutal and sanguinary instincts would triumph, leading to the despotism of the masses, or paving the way for a military dictatorship.

By contrast, the social radical tendency within the United Irishmen sympathised with the poor. While acknowledging their degradation, they also recognised their inherent humanity and their possession of the rights of man. In the Irish context, they were heirs to a humiliating history of vicious dispossession and a grinding government (in this sense, the United Irishmen rejected not the Irish past but the British [or colonial] past in Ireland). In figures like Russell, Tone, McCracken and Sampson, the United Irishmen reached out to the poor, and especially the despised Catholic poor. In so doing, they connected with the view of poverty internalised in the popular consciousness, articulated with emotional energy in the scalding anger of a Cox or Taaffe. A further legacy of a colonial situation was the precocious establishment of a 'national' consciousness among the Irish Catholic poor. Living alongside the settlers, and being at the receiving end of the colonising process accelerated their precocious transition into political consciousness. From the seventeenth century onwards, the island's indigenous 'peasants' had already been turned into Irishmen; their well developed consciousness of a national identity differentiated the Irish poor from their European counterparts, who generally had to await the intrusion of centralised nation-states before advancing to this stage.

These contrasting attitudes to poverty also issued in contrasting attitudes to the concept of popular revolution. The 'moderates' favoured a French invasion to ensure discipline, not trusting the Irish poor to rise above a vengeful jacquerie. The more advanced radicals gradually moved to contemplation of an insurrection without French assistance, trusting to the revolutionary potential and discipline of the Irish poor. By late 1796, as Tone's adroit diplomacy in Paris began to reap tangible dividends from a receptive anglophobic Directory, the emerging debate over insurrectionary strategy began to clarify and harden. If an external strategy was pursued, then the east Ulster movement could mobilise in strong support of a French landing in Lough Foyle or Lough Swilly. If an internal strategy was the favoured option, then the Ulster strength was misplaced. The decisive blow would be struck in Dublin and the organisational base of the movement would have to be shifted to the capital and its hinterland, if necessary, at the expense of the morale and momentum of the Ulster organisation.

The government and conservatives had not been idle while these developments occurred within the radical movement. Stymied by the anticipation and actuality of the Fitzwilliamite Lord Lieutenancy, the conservatives had marked time in late 1794 and early 1795, as the reorganisation of the United Irishmen proceeded. But once English (Fitzwilliam) and Irish (Grattan) whigs had been seen off, the conservatives tightened their grip again. A revamped security emphasis can be detected – the initiation of organised intelligence gathering, the toughening and centralisation of law enforcement, the first officially approved deviation from the rule-of-law in the Carhampton campaign against Defenders in the north midlands, the initially covert and later overt support for the newly-established Orange Order, the eventual endorsement of a yeomanry ('arming the Protestants that can be depended upon') – all these were responses to the rapidly deteriorating

security situation in 1795–1796.[16] The wily Fitzgibbon spelled out to the obtuse Camden the necessarily explicit sectarianism of the new policy in September 1796.

> In the very critical situation of this country, beset as we are by the treason of one set of men [presbyterians] and the barbarism of another [catholics], I cannot but think that it will be dangerous in the extreme to damp the ardour of those who may be depended upon, under an apprehension that their zeal may become the subject of misrepresentation by the catholics, who I will freely own to your Excellency are in my opinion the body of all others in this country at the present moment who ought to be watched most narrowly, if a foreign enemy were to make a descent.[17]

Edward Cooke, another key player with Fitzgibbon, Foster and Beresford, noted the dangerous security situation in November 1796:

> The North very bad. In Antrim and the borders of Tyrone, Derry and Down, not a man will come forwards or take the oath of allegiance. The United Irishmen boast they have 150,000 sworn, including Defenders ... Let no man act or think upon any other ground except that part of the north of Ireland is in the most dangerous smothered rebellion, the more quiet, the more hostile.[18]

The immediate response to Bantry Bay on the conservative side was to heave a collective sigh of relief. The Protestant wind had once more delivered Ireland out of the clutches of its ancient enemy and West Munster had remained gratifyingly placid while the French ships tossed on the anxious Bantry waves. But the initial relief soon subsided once the considerable downside became apparent. The army had been unwieldly, inefficient and suicidally slow to mobilise. Writing in January 1797, John Beresford reflected on the acute devastation which Bantry Bay inflicted on the received wisdom on security policy.

> [The French fleet] has truly alarmed every thinking man in the nation. We see that in a like situation we must depend upon

ourselves and are we prepared? Two days after they were at anchor at Bantry, we had less than 3,000 men, 2 pieces of artillery, and no magazine of any kind, no firing, no hospital, no provision etc. etc. No landing was made. Providence prevented it. If there had, where was a stand to be made? It is clear that Cork was gone. Who could answer afterwards for the loyalty of the country then in possession of the French?[19]

Salt was rubbed in those wounds by opposition figures like Henry Grattan:

The circumstance of the French fleet escaping two British fleets, riding triumphantly for seventeen days, and getting back unmolested, formed a phenomenon in the naval history of Great Britain, which challenges enquiry. The plea urged in excuse, that the Admiralty was not acquainted with the destination of the French fleet, was a great aggravation of the neglect.[20]

For the more intelligent conservatives, the conclusion was clear. Ireland must depend on itself alone for its internal security, and should seize the security initiative, independent of London input. John Lees, conservative insider, made the point to Lord Auckland that British interference, notably in the precipitous repeal of the Penal Laws against the advice of Dublin, had destabilised Ireland, and that, in future, the handling of Irish affairs should be left to the discretion of Irish politicians, who alone knew the real nature of the problem.[21] A further conclusion was that the expanded military capacity of the Irish state (militia, yeomanry, fencible regiments) should now be forcefully deployed in robust counter-insurgency measures, before the French landed again.

A long memorandum from Cooke to Auckland in February clearly detailed the alarming situation now facing the Irish cabinet:

We expect a second attack: Bonaparte's success must give new spirits, and I have this day an account from Brest of the 19th stating that measures for a second expedition were in activity ... We have a good but inexperienced army of near 40,000, officers included, and 30,000 yeomanry in drill – a force nearly sufficient, if well conducted, well disposed, well officered, well generalled. But here we fail. I own myself that, from the beginning of the war to the present hour, I have seen nothing of military system here or in England ... But we have the laziness of an old and perishing system about us. We want a general who can give confidence ... We expect Hoche and Vendean and Pyrenean armies and all their good artillerists and generals. Whom have we to oppose them? Lord Carhampton, quick but flighty, unexperienced, unsystematic. Dalrymple of the old school, but unwieldy, and incapable of great exertion. Smith, busy, confused, wild, mad. Yet 'tis on these we depend. The public wants a general on [sic] whom they can have confidence, who they know can manage and fight 25,000 men. We have not the man, and the public are in despair ... The object of the enemy is Cork. If in possession of Cork, they get an impregnable harbour, and they will be able to fortify the town. England is lost if Cork be taken. And it was within six hours of being lost. Count not on our loyalty. We follow the strongest. The principle is fully as much in favour of France as of England in the south, and in the north entirely French ... We shall I fear be in troubled waters. The respectable catholics will come forward modestly, the violent are caballing for reform, the north are really disaffected presbyterian republicans. Our atmosphere varies with French successes.[22]

One implication was very clear. The Irish conservatives would henceforth have to shift for themselves in dealing with the security threat. Cooke had been horrified by the inadequacy of the British response when the Bantry crisis was at its height:

It is shocking to reflect that the army of Great Britain is now so circumstanced that, except with cavalry and the Guards, it could not send a man to Ireland. This should be remedied. There is much murmur against the admiralty for suffering a French fleet to ride in the Irish ports unmolested for three weeks.[23]

An immediate response was to alter the relative weight assigned to the internal and external threat. The cleft stick of Irish security had been that no single policy could effectively address both threats simultaneously. A French (external) threat could only be met by systematic troop concentrations, permanently deployed in fixed camps for strategic reasons. The concept would be to create two flexible lines, which could

quickly seal in Ulster along the line of the Erne and the drumlin belt, and Munster, along a line from Limerick to Waterford
Harbour. The domestic threat (low-level insurgency by the
Defenders and United Irishmen) could only be met by a policy
of dispersal, often in ad hoc fashion in response to frantic local
pleas. Pursuing the domestic agenda, less than one-fifth of
40,000 troops were concentrated in camps in the summer of
1796. In December, with the French fleet nosing north through
the fog, troops were promiscuously scattered in 71 locations; in
County Cork, 4,702 troops manned 14 different locations, some
in detachments as small as 100.[24]

TABLE I: TROOPS IN COUNTY CORK, DECEMBER 1796

Cork Harbour	582	Bantry	240
Dunmanway	540	Millstreet	150
Bandon	520	Macroom	100
Enniskeane	500	Drimoleague	100
Clonakilty	500	Rathcormack	100
Cork City	490	Kilworth	100
Skibbereen	350		

The advent of this formidable French fleet of 25 ships and
15,000 well armed and battle-hardened veterans shattered the
basis of this response. Almost as a reflex, Carhampton's initial
response to Bantry had been to worry about Ulster, warning
General Knox 'to keep in awe with an iron-hand such of the ill-
disposed inhabitants of the north who may presume to take
advantage of the enemy's attack.'[25] But the implications quickly sank in: if the celebrated wooden walls of England could be
breached so spectacularly, then a recurrence became not just
possible but likely, and an entirely fresh security policy had to
be implemented. This dictated the concentration of regular
troops in permanent camps, like Blaris Moor, Lehunstown and
Ardfinnan, leaving the local situation to be dealt with by the
militia and especially the yeomanry.

The popular response to the French fleet was widespread.
Writing from Antrim on 10 January, George MacCartney was
chagrined that the response to a request for a show of loyalty
had been 'a sullen discontent' and 'an aversion to taking the

109

oath of allegiance.' He claimed that 'the countenances of the lower sort of people were filled with joy on hearing of the approach of the French fleet and full of sorrow when it was reported that the English fleet had come up with them.'[26] From County Kildare, Mary Leadbeater noted how the French fleet 'caused a ferment in the minds of the people,'[27] while further south in Wexford, Miles Byrne registered general disappointment: 'I shall never forget the mournful silence, the consternation of the poor people at the different chapels on Christmas Day and the following Sunday, after learning that the French had not landed and that the French fleet had returned to France.'[28] A flurry of letters from Hugh White of Clady in County Antrim offer a revealing insight into rank-and-file United Irish thinking in Ulster. He was reassured by the leadership and quality of the French troops that appeared at Bantry Bay.

> The French are all picked desperate men who are embarked with General Hock. They fought against the Vendian's and despot priests. They will fight with the Presbyterians if any other [i.e., the Catholics] would offer to retreat and turn wrong.

White then observed that 'we expect another visit more decisive,' and that 'the north is said by old prophecys' to be the next place 'they will land after Bantry.' He reported that 'we have now no religious animosities' because 'the brogue and bonnet are all United.' Despite government oppression (United Irishmen jailed 'without any tryal or even oath', 'arming of the Orangemen or midnight robbers and burners, [who] are completely organised and officered by government hacks', the raising of yeomen as 'footstools of tyranny,' the government's wish 'to use Belfast like the McDonalds of Glenco'), the United Irishmen could still muster 600,000 against 100,000 loyalists (militia, yeomen, Orangemen, and Scotch and English fencibles). As a result, White was 'waiting patiently for the opening of the great drama which will usher in a new scene to unborn millions, tho' millions may and perhaps will fall in establishing the foundations on which it will be built.' And the government (already 'put to their wit's end' and 'in much fear and terror' and despite their 'straining every nerve to dragoon the people into the lowest vassilage'), was doomed, because 'the multitude have a mind to take down the landlords and tyrannic great men.'[29]

For the United Irishmen leadership, the advent of the French presented two quandaries. One was the apparent indifference of the local people, the second was the issue of what would have been the outcome of a successful French invasion. The quiescence of West Munster could be explained away in a number of ways. The Cork area was saturated with troops. There was no sharp divide in either city or county parliamentary politics due to the dominance of the Shannon interest. Neither was there a divide on the Catholic issue – elsewhere, a potent recruiting ground for the United Irishmen. There was no guild tradition in Cork, unlike Dublin, to act as a seed bed of radicalism and most crucially of all, Cork United Irishmen activists were largely Dublin-based – Arthur O'Connor, the Sheares brothers, Richard Dry, John Daly Burk. Others sought an explanation in West Cork's remoteness, its Irish-speaking populace and its adherence to the 'old' Whiteboy rather than to the 'new' United Irishmen radicalism.

The second issue was more intractable. Would the French have landed as equal partners in revolution or as arrogant conquerors? The rampages of the French army outside the hexagon – in Belgium, in Holland, the Rhineland and Italy – were well known, as was the way in which the betrayed radicals of those countries had turned against their French overlords. There had been an obvious shift in French policy – not exporting revolution, but expanding France to its 'natural' frontiers to safeguard the permanency of the revolution within France. Would the French not be equally self-serving in Ireland, installing a pliant puppet regime, bleeding it white in requisitions and then cynically abandoning it for selfish reasons in subsequent negotiations with Britain? In 1796, the rapacious progress of Napoleon in Italy did not offer a comforting parallel for Ireland. To moderate United Irish leaders, the great attraction of the French would be their ability to discipline popular insurgency in Ireland, otherwise potentially unmanageable. To more radical leaders, like O'Connor, Fitzgerald and Neilson, the French solution looked less attractive as France began to show unmistakable signs of autocracy, despotism and imperial ambition. By the end of 1796, there were signs of unease about the French connection, signified in anxious attempts to clarify the level of payments, the powers and composition of a transitional government and the size of the French force, in an effort to retain control of the revolution in United Irishmen hands, and to set precise limits to French ambitions.

The internal debate intensified after Bantry Bay. A French incursion was no longer theoretical and distant, but proximate and pragmatic. Copious conservative propaganda publicised the harsh treatment by the French of their supposed allies.[30] The insistent question then became: what was the point of merely exchanging a British for a French despotism? The solution was to develop the indigenous strategy in tandem with the French option: rather than a paper army of sympathisers who would support the French, the United Irishmen needed a disciplined secret army. Rather than Ulster, the movement needed to be strong in Leinster. Bantry Bay accelerated the adoption of the indigenous strategy. Dublin now became the crucial organisational target, plus the inner crescent of surrounding counties – Meath, Kildare and Wicklow – and an outer crescent from Westmeath to Wexford. The best field operatives – MacCabe, Hope, Metcalfe – were withdrawn from Ulster and set to work to build the Leinster organisation.[31]

Ironically, the frightened conservatives, humiliated and haunted by Bantry, decided to unleash a wave of terror on the Ulster United Irishmen in the spring of 1797 – unaware that the strategic goalposts were shifting. The 'dragooning of Ulster' is usually taken to signal the end of effective United Irishmen organisation there, in the aftermath of large-scale arrests and the roughing-up of Down and Armagh. Remarkably, this onslaught left the Dublin and embryonic Leinster organisation unscathed, and in a sense masked the changing geography of the United Irishmen movement. Strategists like Lord Edward Fitzgerald were also carefully monitoring troop dispositions.

After Bantry Bay, the troops had been concentrated across South Ulster and Munster to be rapidly deployed in the event of a renewed French attempt. Given the prevailing westerlies and the bottleneck configuration of the Irish Sea, no one ever entertained the possibility that an invasion fleet would attempt the east coast, where they could be easily immobilised by the wind, and trapped within the narrow entrances. The government's troop deployment therefore virtually ignored Leinster – with the exception of a large camp at Lehunstown outside Bray.

The revised United Irishmen plan was tailored to suit these circumstances. The Dublin organisation would rise independently, supported by a converging inner crescent. The outer crescent would seal the Dublin insurrection off from troop concentrations in the south-west and north. The Wicklow men would insert themselves between Lehunstown and the capital, and the city organisation would then have only the much derided yeomanry to oppose them – corpulent lawyers, flashy Trinity students, and a rag, tag and bobtail of placemen and opportunists. Unburdened by Ulster's ideological commitment to Volunteering and inveterate hostility to the yeomanry concept, the Leinster radicals also systematically infiltrated yeomanry corps, acquiring valuable training, weapons, and intelligence. A further advantage of the new strategy was limited gentry opposition in the predominantly Whig counties of Kildare (Fitzgerald) and Wicklow (Fitzwilliam) and a divided security response in Wexford and Carlow.

Although wary about the practical impact of a successful French invasion, the United Irishmen were buoyed up by one aspect of Bantry Bay – the incompetent government response. One of their pamphlets mocked: 'Who was to prevent the French landing? A handful of half-starved Scotch Cullies, many of whom on hearing of the French name, were already panic-stricken. Some were frost-bitten. Others tired on the roads, for they went by forced marches. Others for self-preservation lay down and died in peace.' The pamphlet derided the loyalists who only 'evinced proofs of their spaniel spirit and fawning fondness on this occasion to a government that

113

returned their kindness by kicks.'[32] A further result of Bantry Bay was to make the United Irishmen an attractive option. Many hitherto uncommitted or wavering now joined the radicals, seemingly unstoppable in their momentum. James Hope, for example, noted how even the reticent wealthy joined up after Bantry Bay.[33] In May 1797, a Cork-based pamphleteer (Arthur O'Connor?) operating under the guise of loyalism, offered a bleak picture of Ireland: 'It presents the most alluring prospect of invasion.' It was 'humiliating to perceive that the British fleet alone is looked up to as the only palladium of our safety' because 'no reliance whatsoever can be placed upon the naval force which defends our coast.' And if the French landed, the loyalty of the ordinary people could not be assumed, because seven-eighths of them were 'deplorably miserable' and in a worse condition than any of the peasantries of the 'despotic states' of Europe. They were also now aware of their enslaved condition because of 'the spirit of democracy and equality of rights and privileges which the American and French revolutions have rendered the favourite topics of discussion among the lower classes of people.'[34]

The United Irishmen also sought simultaneously to undermine confidence in the yeomanry and army. In describing the dragooning of Ulster, they claimed that 'the blood-hounds of despotism' had been 'let loose against us ... in a worse than oriental despotism.' But the soldiers were not fighting for principle: they were 'mercenary tools, the livery servants of the faction, the Janizaries of a traitor junta.' The yeomen officers were toy soldiers – 'young, giddy coxcombs desirous of sporting their dear persons in military uniform.' They could not command respect or affection because they were an illegitimate gentry: 'Are we then to fall prey to the scum and dregs of the creation – the upstart mushroom growth of a night, whose ancestors within the memory of man never aspired beyond the lower dispensations to which they were born – brewers, servants, mowers, common soldiers, etc.'[35] In his challenging 'Address to the free electors of Antrim,' Arthur O'Connor made the wider European point that he would never support 'a war that has been undertaken for the destruction of liberty abroad,

114

and for the preservation of corruption at home.' 'For this,' he claimed, 'attempts have been made to arm Irishmen against Irishmen, and the genius of the fiend which supplied the monsters of France with pretences for massacre, after desolating La Vendée, has made its appearance in Armagh.'[36]

The first half of 1797, then, as well as United Irishmen reorganisation and the deployment of the transformed military capacity of the state against them, also witnessed intense high political activity, in preparation for the summer general election. In April and May, there were stridently anti-government county meetings in Armagh, Antrim and Down, calling for the resignation of ministers. A similar meeting, requisitioned by 6,000 freeholders, in Kildare was proclaimed, precipitating the withdrawal of the radicals and Whigs (including Grattan) from parliament. The Whigs eventually refused to contest the election – notably in the two most radical counties of Kildare and Down.

Alarmed by this tense political situation, the government intensified its efforts to regain control of east Ulster. In the spring of 1797, even loyalists like Charles Warburton of Armagh were demonstrating extreme fear:

> The game is nearly up in the north – no juries, no prosecutions, no evidence against any person under the denomination of *united man!* The men of property and clergy completely alarmed and, instead of resistance, are all flying away into garrisons towns.[37]

Appalled conservatives called for a tougher line against the United Irishmen: 'The people is nothing more than a ferocious untameable tiger which may sometimes be indulged by lengthening his chain, but never with perfect liberty'.[38] The government response was to stage-manage a theatre of terror, designed to intimidate the recalcitrant masses: the dragooning of Ulster which involved 10,000 troops under the hardline General Lake, the grafting of the Orange Order onto the yeomanry, the show trial and execution of four Monaghan Militia men at Blaris Moor, the military suppression of the *Northern Star*, the execution of William Orr – all reflected the 'get tough' policies initiated by Bantry Bay and accelerated by the Spithead mutiny which immobilised the British fleet. London, furious at these two potentially catastrophic imperial incidents, encouraged Dublin Castle in an unrestrained use of force. General John Knox in Ulster caught the prevailing mood in June 1797: 'The country can never be settled until it is disarmed and that is only to be done by terror.'[39] Another army officer, Lord Blayney, reported from south Armagh, where in one night he had burned 22 houses, personally cut down a suspect, and ordered 300 lashes for another suspect: 'It is useless crowding the gaols. If you are disengaged and will take a trip down, you may see some amusement with the natives.'[40]

Faced with these policies, Henry Grattan argued that 'the best manufacturer of an Irish Jacobin is a British minister' and he questioned the conservative analysis: 'They think they are strong because they have gotten every man who loves a bribe and hates a papist ... Aided by religious discord, government wishes to draw a line of separation between the gentry and the people.'[41] Even a militia officer on duty in south Armagh was moved to complain: 'The depredations committed all around here are shocking to humanity by what they call Orange Boys. It is done by the sanction of government. Were I to enumerate the robberies, murders and shameful outrages committed on the Catholics of this place by those Orange Boys, headed by officers in full yeomanry uniform, it would be an endless business.'[42]

In the face of these provocations, the United Irishmen urged their members to maintain discipline and unity of purpose, and to trust the strength of their own organisation.

Trouble not yourselves, whether France is to send 40 or 50,000 troops here; whether England is to send 40 or 50,000 troops here; but turn your attention to Ireland – think of what she was, what she is, and what she may be. Think that were you to divide, as in former days, and one part to seek protection and assistance from one of those powerful nations, the other party from the other nation, what carnage and rivers of blood would ensue – slavery would follow, and Ireland be undone, perhaps for ever. But in your UNION is your safety – in Union is your strength, your importance, and your liberty. In whatever scale your weight is cast it will preponderate in an instant. He is your enemy, and the man of blood who would divide you – he is your friend, and the man of peace, who would keep you together.[43]

By mid 1797, the United Irishmen were making rapid advances in Dublin, aided by the war-accentuated misery of the traditionally volatile working class. Barbara Verschoyle, the Dublin agent of the Fitzwilliam estate, reported in May 1797:

This war has made millions miserable – the multitudes of poor destroyed manufacturers that are daily in the streets exhibited such scenes of woe as are really shocking to humanity. The stopage of the circulation of cash has occasioned a great part of this distress as almost all the manufactures have stopped and I am told several parts of the country remain uncultivated. In the North I am told there is not 1/3 of the flax sown that used to be. What must be the consequences of all this – since wretchedness seems to stare every one in the face – yet nothing is doing to employ the poor – no money to be had and how can it be expected that they will quietly starve? The poor man that on Saturday night used to bring to his little family the honest earnings of the week is now unemployed himself and his once happy family are starving – should he fly from them to seek by robbery and murder for the means to get them bread sure it is not to be wondered at. Then how can this country be quiet where so many thousands are unemployed, where so many millions are starving, and where this wretchedness is daily increasing and only to be relieved by Death.[44]

From Dublin, emissaries made their way into the surrounding counties, and the organisation continued to gather momentum in Kildare, Wicklow, Wexford and Carlow. The Dublin strategy dictated the necessity of the United Irish leadership refusing the urgent appeals from Ulster to rise immediately in the summer of 1797. The leadership wished to put the organisational capacity in place to deliver the decisive blow in the capital, which required patient recruitment and mobilisation in Leinster. In one sense, the pressure on Ulster drew Dublin Castle's attention away from their own backyard and the Leinster organisation remained inviolate until the fateful meeting at Oliver Bond's house on 12 March 1798.

By late 1797, even in hitherto quiescent Cork, the United Irishmen organisation began to spread rapidly: it lacked, however, significant leaders, with the exception of John Sweeney. His powerful 'Address to the patriots of Imokilly' meeting at 'Liberty Green' at Cloyne in October reflected a determined effort to fuse the older Whiteboy/Rightboy and newer radical traditions, to politicise poverty, and to develop a comparative framework.[45] Sweeney addressed the crucial Munster issue of tithes – explicitly referring to Captain Right:

> Resolved that the tythe of potatoes not being demanded in other parts of this nation, & being the chief support of the poor of this country, we solemnly pledge ourselves to each other not to pay the same, and to do all in our power to hinder and obstruct the sd. tythe of being paid.

Sweeney updated the agenda by linking tithes to a state-sponsored church, exorbitant church livings and rapacious proctors – all to be abolished under a revolutionary dispensation which would separate church and state. He also focused on excessive rents, fuelled by oppressive landlords and land-grabbers: he denounced the war-inflated price of provisions, and the consequent loss of milk from the already borderline diet of the poor, as a result of which 'the poor wretches of this country are reduced to a state of degradation below that of the negroes of the West-Indies.' Sweeney's arguments and rhetoric echo those of his countryman John Burk (*The Cry of the Poor for Bread*), while resonating powerfully with the existing agrarian and Jacobite traditions. This potent fusion can also be seen in the attraction of the poet Micheál Óg Ó Longáin to the United Irish cause. Local and historically rooted grievances are now, for the first time, being articulated in national and inter-national terms, and linked to an explicit project for political and if necessary revolutionary change. The United Irishmen were therefore the crucial bridge between Jacobitism and Jacobinism for the Irish poor. It was this novel political sensibility ('educated Whiteboyism' as another Munster man, John Fitzgibbon described it) which faced the sectarian state as the rebellion of 1798 approached.

Set in this wider chronological and geographical frame, Bantry Bay can be seen as a watershed event, bisecting and realigning the trajectories of both the revolutionary and counter-revolutionary movements of the 1790s. Once the French were on the sea, in such formidable numbers, everything changed. The threat was to remain intact until the final surrender of Napoleon. In terms which took account of the gravity of the French scenario, Hugh Dorrian sardonically commented:

> No wonder the English took good care of the wonderful hero after he surrendered to them, for by that act, he relieved them of many a restless day and sleepless night. Such was their dread whilst 'Bony' conquered that if an extraordinary large seagull's wing appeared on the horizon, it was in the hurry of the moment taken for French canvas, and the telescope was adjusted.[46]

119

THE FRENCH ARE ON THE SAY'

Gearóid Ó Crualaoich

A French invasion fleet *did* arrive at Bantry Bay in December
1796. The significance of this event in terms of history and politics is being thoroughly explored by other contributors. I wish
to consider its symbolic and mythic significance in the contexts
both of the popular culture of the 1790s and the folklore record
of succeeding times. Two aspects of the popular culture of the
1790s that are most relevant are 1) traditions of a heroic liberator coming to the aid of the native population and leading
them in a final battle in which the old order is restored; 2) the
tradition of the personification of Ireland and of Irish
sovereignty as an abused and abandoned royal female figure
in thrall to a foreign usurper. These traditions had found characteristic eighteenth century expression in prophecies, in legends and in verse form and were one prominent feature of the
popular world view existing in the Ireland of the late eighteenth century within whose horizon the French invasion fleet
appeared. The folklore record of succeeding times is very meagre in respect of the events at Bantry Bay of December 1796. We
have, on the one hand, oral traditions of eyewitness evidence
of the French presence and, on the other, folk legend narratives
that recount the event within a traditional paradigm which
emphasises a continuing ecclesiastical authority in the popular
domain and a patriarchal repulsing by that ecclesiastical authority of outside, and possibly female challenge.

To begin with, we can look at two pieces of eyewitness lore
that remind us of how vividly oral tradition can transmit the
actuality of historical events. Recalling listening to an old man
in County Longford describing so vividly the incidents that
took place there at the time of the French invasion of 1798,
Frank O'Connor once wrote that 'I had to pull myself together
and remind myself that it was not this old man who had seen

them, but his grandfather'.[1] Something of this emotional charge that seems to telescope time can be sensed in both pieces of eyewitness lore concerning Bantry. The first piece is recorded by C. J. F. MacCarthy, where he quotes a Cork resident whose mother, a native of the Drimoleague area, 'could recall her grandfather telling her how, when a child, his father had carried him up Deelish to see the French ships down in Bantry Bay during Christmas 1796'.[2] Deelish is the name of a district to the north-west of Drimoleague from where one can see down over the inner part of Bantry Bay and Mr Mac-Carthy's informant told how local people gathered to see the French in the bay between 22 December, 1796 and the end of the first week of the New Year of 1797. One might think that the memory of this would be prominent in the local tradition of the Deelish area in general and yet there does not appear to be any trace of it in the historical lore reported in 1937–8 to the Irish Folklore Commission from the schools of that area – or (indeed) of other strategic locations such as Durrus, Adrigole or Dursey – as part of the Commission's Schools' Collections project. We can see here evidence of the individually and communally selective nature of oral tradition which is far more vulnerable to revision and reinterpretation by those transmitting it across the generations than is the documentary record. This point will be considered further in relation to the folk legends of Bantry '96 to be discussed below.

The second piece of eyewitness lore concerns not events in Bantry Bay itself but their repercussion in terms of military activity in the hinterland of Cork city. A Mr Eoghan Lane, a farmer of Berrings, near Inniscarra, who was aged 84 years in 1938 told Seán Ua Cróinín, collector for the Irish Folklore Commission, that he remembered

My grandmother, who was ninety-six years of age when she died, and she is dead now close on sixty years, telling me that she remembered going into Cork with her father when she was about twelve years of age and, as they were going along the road, the army of soldiers came along from Cork, out, and as they were told after they passed, that they were going on to Bantry – that the French invasion was in there.[3]

121

Seán Ua Cróinín records Eoghan Lane as reporting that his grandmother was living at Berrings at the time when she told him of her memories of seeing the troops on the move west but it is not stated where she lived at the earlier time of her actual childhood encounter with the troop movement. We can, I imagine, take it that this was also in the western hinterland of Cork city and that what we have from her, via the verbal account from her grandson, is eyewitness evidence of the marching out from Cork to Bandon of the company of Fencible soldiers to which Tom Bartlett has referred from the historical record.

Both pieces of eyewitness lore, or both 'memorates' to use the technical folklore term, attest to the fact that in December of 1796 the French invasion 'was in'. What, we may ask, was, as a result of this, likely to come ashore at Bantry at that time? A variety of answers is possible in accordance with the various world views of those witnessing the event and hearing of it then or later. For the likes of the inhabitants of Seafield, later Bantry House, it was anarchy and revolution that were likely to come ashore; for the United Irishmen it was the forces of Reason and the European Enlightenment; for many of the Irish-speaking majority of the ordinary people of the south-west coast, it would have seemed the imminent fulfilment of millenarian prophecy and Jacobite poetic imaginings regarding the restoration of the true order of things, metaphysical as well as political, in the coming ashore of the messianic forces of Liberation.

IT IS OF INTEREST TO examine the origins of this last, essentially conservative popular vision of the significance of the French in the Bay and to note the ironic contrast between this majority conservatism of apprehension and the radical modernity of apprehension and expectation on the part of the United Irishmen minority in their estimation of the meaning of the approach of the Hoche armada to the south-western coast. If the French invasion was, in United Irishman terms, the application to the Irish body politic of a forward-looking Enlightenment ideology of liberty and equality for all citizens, it also

122

represented, in the ideology of popular culture as expressed in the prophecies and poetry of one brand of ancestral tradition, a move towards the regressive restoration of a medieval ordering of society in accordance with archaic notions of kingship and royal sovereignty that underlay the Jacobite poetry of eighteenth century Gaelic Munster. I want to suggest that there was (and is) a yet further way of perceiving the significance and the potential – at symbolic and mythic level – of the French forces in Bantry Bay and that this further kind of perception, while still congruent with the Enlightenment perspective on the 'invasion', connects to yet another brand of Irish ancestral tradition that is very different from that of the patriarchal mythology which envisages the liberation of a hapless Mother Ireland sovereignty queen figure by some hero from over the water. First however it is necessary to examine the nature of both the Heroic Liberator and the Sovereignty Queen paradigms.

The Sovereignty Queen figure is associated with the symbolism and the ritual of an archaic notion of 'sacred marriage', the *hieros gamos*, that is widespread throughout Indo-European cultures. The central motif of this conception is that a rightful king is wedded to the territory of his kingdom – in the person of the supernatural female who constitutes the royal and divine personification of the territory in question. The corollary of such rightful union of mortal king and immortal divine bride is the prosperity of land and people – a state of affairs that is thought to last while the king himself remains righteous and unblemished. Should he deliver false judgement, should he become disabled physically or – worst of all – should he be displaced by some usurping stranger, in violation of the sacred marriage bond, then a blighted and wasted landscape, in which nothing thrives, will mirror the sorrowful state to which such circumstances reduce the divine female personification of the kingdom's territory. This myth of a Sovereignty Queen as divine spouse of the lawful king was widely used in the political propaganda with which competing Irish royal lineages pressed their claims for the recognition of their supremacy in the early medieval period.

The Uí Néill, for instance, in their northern supremacy and the Uí Bhriain in their supremacy in north Munster, both invoke the figure of the Sovereignty Queen in stories that locate their own assumption of political legitimacy in a mythic encounter with the divine female agency on the part of their founding ancestors – encounters that saw the Sovereignty Goddess confer primacy on the particular lineage – O'Neill or O'Brien – and pledge it for succeeding generations. The Sovereignty Queen myth in early medieval Ireland is thus a device of political propaganda indulged within the cultural worlds both of the political and literary elites and of popular tradition. Later on, with the development of different conceptions of the Irish nation and of national sovereignty, the figure of the divine Sovereignty Queen continues to occupy a very prominent position in the (at once) literary and popular firmament constructed and cultivated by poets of ancestral disposition. By the eighteenth century, in the aftermath of the overthrow of the royal house of Stuart and its replacement by the house of Orange, the literati of Gaelic Ireland, and particularly of Munster had developed a variety of Vision or *Aisling* poetry in which a forlorn female figure appears to the poet and, on questioning, identifies herself as Ireland mourning the loss of her rightful royal spouse and seeking deliverance from the thralldom in which she finds herself. Such a symbolic figure looms large in the late eighteenth century popular imagination on which the events of Bantry Bay 1796 impinge.

The chief potential Heroic Deliverer of *Aisling*-type poetry is the leader of the House of Stuart who is envisaged as coming as Liberator from over-the-water to set things to rights. As such, Bonnie Prince Charles, *An Séarlas Óg*, is but the latest in a long line of Liberator/Deliverers whose symbolic lineage stretches back in Irish myth and literature to as equally archaic an origin as that of the Sovereignty Queen. In fact it may be asserted that the divine hero *Lugh* – himself the mythic prototype of the rightful king – is the original Deliverer in the role he plays in the story of the Battle of Moytura (*Cath Maige Tuired*) – the paradigmatic Final Showdown of ancestral myth – wherein the supremacy of the native order was recounted

124

and asserted by the medieval literati. Just as the political contests between early medieval Irish lineages for supremacy utilised the ancient figure of the divine Sovereignty Queen, so too use was made of the ancient figure of the Heroic Deliverer in ways that associated him with the interests of specific political factions within the native order.

The figure of *Aodh Eangach* is one such mythic figure, developed in the course of ninth century Uí Néill struggles for political supremacy. *Aodh Eangach* becomes the potential Deliverer of the Uí Néill from their oppressors and it was alleged that his coming had been foretold centuries earlier by Saint Bearchán. It is, incidentally, in association with the figure of Aodh Eangach – the warrior saviour of the Uí Néill – that the symbolic Red Hand develops which became the talisman of northern political allegiance and identity. *Aodh Eangach* himself and other mythic potential Deliverers of the Uí Néill are envisaged as having the mark of victorious slaughter visible on their bodies – the bloodied hand signifying that Great Battle, the final, showdown battle, in which the enemies and oppressors of the Uí Néill are to be overthrown and repulsed. In later Uí Néill praise poetry and vision poetry (*Aisling*) the great leader who will bring them triumph over their enemies is called *Crobhdhearg* – the red-clawed or red-handed one.

While no one in the Bantry Bay area in the 1790s would have mistaken the imminent arrival of Tone and a French liberation army as the coming of a *Lugh* or an *Aodh Eangach* or a *Crobhdhearg* to provide prophesied deliverance, nevertheless the continuing availability in popular ideology of just such an expectation of overseas deliverance and its flowering in Munster Jacobite popular verse towards the end of the eighteenth century is evident. Two examples of the application of such an idea, examples from the 1590s and the 1690s, are relevant ones. Hugh O'Neill, the Earl of Tyrone, in open rebellion against Elizabeth the First, was said by his poet, prior to the Battle of the Yellow Ford in 1598, to be engaging in the final showdown battle prophesied by Bearchán. We cannot know for sure the influence of that poet's pronouncement on the mood of O'Neill's troops but O'Neill was, as we know, victorious in battle on that occasion.

In the 1690s an Irish-born officer of the Spanish army arrived into Ireland a few days after the Battle of the Boyne and joined the retreating Jacobite forces. This man was an O'Donnell with the rank of earl and the reputation of being marked on his body with the red sign of the messianic saviour of his people. The *Ball Dearg* or Red Spot, a similar prophetic mark to that of the Red Hand, was an item of popular belief widely known and understood and it was as *Ball Dearg Ó Domhnaill*, as Heroic Deliverer from-over-the-water, that this O'Donnell participated prominently in what was popularly perceived to be another Final Battle – at Singland during the Siege of Limerick. Victory did not, on this occasion, attend the efforts of *Ball Dearg* and, having avoided engagement at the subsequent and even more disastrous Battle of Aughrim, he changed sides, fought in the Williamite cause at Sligo and was the recipient, on his return to Spain, of a Williamite pension until his death in 1704.

Another century on, in the 1790s, the Stuart Pretender is the figure who fills the role, in Munster popular Liberation ideology, of the Hero from across the sea who will come to the aid of Ireland and her stricken people. This Jacobite allegorical belief and expectation endures in Munster vernacular literature and in the popular culture of the south-west at the end of the eighteenth century despite the kind of class development in Munster society of which David Dickson speaks;[4] despite growing bilingualism, despite spreading literacy, despite increasing participant experience in the rapidly modernising world; despite, even – in poet Eoghan Rua Ó Súilleabháin's case, at least – active service in the British Navy. This conviction that help would arrive from over the water to restore the old order and rout the enemy oppressor would seem, in a sense (a sense we can surmise as having a lively existence in the minds of many) to have been answered directly by the arrival of the French fleet into Bantry Bay. Such an occurrence could surely be taken to be the long-prophesied Deliverance, of which, for instance, the poet Seán Clárach Mac Domhnaill had spoken:

Fé mar luadar seandraoithe
do dhéanadh tuar is tairngire
beidh flít i gcuantaibh Bhanba
fá fhéile Shan Sheáin

As the ancient druids mentioned
Who were wont to make prophecy and foretelling
There will come a fleet into the harbours of Ireland
By the midsummer feast day of St John.

We may wish to note, somewhat ironically, no doubt, that the original Hoche/Tone strategy was indeed for a midsummer expedition – and that French naval unreadiness was the reason why the actual date of sailing diverged so far from the one foretold by Seán Clárach and planned for in reality, by Tone, in the first instance.

Another expression of the prominence in oral tradition and folklore of the hope of aid from abroad – and specifically French aid in this instance – is the well-known if anonymous late eighteenth century Whiteboy song of South Tipperary, *Sliabh na mBan*. Reference is made in this song to the imminent arrival of a French fleet who will redress the existing state of affairs.

Tá an Franncach faobhrach lena loingeas gléasta
Agus crannaibh géara acu ar muir le seal
Isé scéal gach éinne go bhfuil a dtriall ar Éirinn
Is go gcuirfid Gaeil bhocht arís ina gceart

The keen French with their fleet under sail
Are standing to sea this while with their elegant masts
It is everyone's story that they are to journey to Ireland
And that they will set to rights again the plight of the poor Gaeil

Yet another powerful expression of such expectation is the famous *Rosc Catha na Mumhan*, a quintessential Munster Jacobite song prophesying the return of the Stuart prince:

Measaim gur subhach don Mhumhain an fhuaim
Is dá maireann go dubhach de chrú na mbuadh
Torann na dtonn le sleasaibh na long

Ag tarraingt go teann 'nár gceann ar cuaird.

I adjudge it a joyful sound for Munster
And for those yet surviving in sorrow of the bloodlines of
    nobility
The beating of the waves on the sides of the ships
That are drawing strongly on to visit us.

In quoting these lines, Maureen Wall reminds us of the role of such songs in both building up and giving expression to the public opinion of the day.[5] Her remarks are worth quoting in full – given their relevance to the apparent fulfilment at Bantry Bay in 1796 of the long-held and fervent expectation of external deliverance:

> It should not be forgotten that the Gaelic poets of the eighteenth century were the pamphleteers and journalists of the Gaelic-speaking multitude. Many a song was sung at a fair or in a tavern or around the firesides .... denouncing local injustice, or reminding the people of their national identity; and prophesying, rather unrealistically, a utopian future, with the Irish language and the Catholic religion high in favour again, when, with the aid of Louis of France, the Stuarts would return to the throne. Those songs helped to build up a public opinion of which the ruling class of the day, and even English-speaking, well-to-do Catholics, were largely unaware.

These country people and especially the Irish-speaking country population of those living on the shores of Bantry Bay at the end of the eighteenth century, would, in Maureen Wall's view, have envisaged a revolution in the wake of a Stuart return, a revolution that would constitute 'a panacea for all their ills' in the re-establishment of the rightful king.

THE ACTUAL REVOLUTION THAT THE arrival of a French fleet into Bantry Bay seemed to presage was a revolution involving, of course, not the restoration of an old order under a rightful royal ruler but the application to the Irish body politic of the ideals and principles of radical Enlightenment ideology as mediated through the French Revolution. The apparently huge gap between the conservative hopes and expectations of the Jacobite tradition and the radically progressive ideology represented by 'the French in the Bay' should however, be seen as itself mediated within Irish popular culture by another kind of vernacular world view than the Jacobite one; a world view that finds its most vigorous expression in the 1789–96 period in the reception afforded in popular cultural tradition to Brian Merriman's poem *Cúirt an Mheáin Oíche*, The Midnight Court. In this poem the central metaphor of the Jacobite *aisling* tradition – the appearance to the poet, in a vision, of the figure of the Sovereignty Queen – is radically transformed in leading not to the passive hope of male deliverance but to the forcefully positive expression of female authority and female power exercised in the cause of female emancipation – and male emancipation too.

Not royal restoration but civil liberation of a democratic and proletarian order is what is imaginatively envisaged and encompassed in Merriman's poem and the resounding oral popularity of the work from its creation in 1780, a full decade and a half before the French in the Bay, is indicative of a radical, progressive, Enlightenment-like tendency in the popular culture of Munster in the 1790s that evokes for us the figure of the Marianne in French popular culture as another female personification – though not of any royal Sovereignty Queen but of the spirit of popular civil emancipation. The unashamed expression of sexuality in the bare-breasted figure of the Marianne and on the part of the chief female protagonists of Merriman's poem represents in either case a symbolically feminist challenge to established patriarchal authority such as can also be seen associated with political and physical subversion in later eighteenth century Ireland. I have in mind here the female disguises and female titles espoused in the rituals and symbols of the Defender and the Whiteboy movements, whose activities were so very often carried on in the names of a Siobhán, or a Sadhbh Olltach, or a Caitlín – appellations of a symbolic female who is the imaginative embodiment not of the Irish nation as much as of an Irish citizenry emergent. I like to think, in this vein, of the French in the Bay as potentially

129

coming to the aid not of the Sean Bhean Bhocht of Jacobite tradition, the Banshee Queen of a moribund and outmoded mentality, but coming rather to further the emancipation of modern men and women and in the setting free of their sexual and imaginative energies in the cause of civil liberty, equality, social and psychic justice.

It is surely relevant to note that even within the later eighteenth century Jacobite *aisling* tradition, the tendency is to give the figure of the female personification of Ireland more proletarian or commoner names than those previously associated with the supernatural royal queen. Rather than being *Eriú* or *Banba* or *Fódhla* or any other of the ancient royal epithets of the Ascendancy Sovereignty Queen, Ireland or, more properly, the Irish citizenry, awaiting deliverance, is given the commoner names of Síle Ní Ghadhra, and Caitlín Triail, Móirín Ní Chuilleanáin and Caitlín Ní Uallacháin, invoking human, flesh and blood women and men and their prospect of living free and equal lives in a renewed civil order freed from social and religious tyranny in line with the ideology of the United Irishman movement that looked to the land of the Marianne for support. In a Thomas Davis lecture on Irish Jacobite Poetry as well as in other of his publications, Breandán Ó Buachalla has asserted that the Jacobite *aisling* tradition is not the regressive, monolithic mind-set it is sometimes made out to be and that it carried into the late eighteenth century a 'powerful millennial message of individual and communal liberation'. Speaking of the popular poetic expression of Jacobite ideology – something we can safely identify as a major formant of the popular world view of the Irish-speaking population in the hinterland of Bantry in 1796, Ó Buachalla says:

> originally a conservative rhetoric imbued with the traditional values of aristocracy, hierarchy, hereditary right and social order, it was also, potentially and eventually, a radical rhetoric in that it foretold, extolled and promoted the overthrow of the existing regime. It must, accordingly, be counted among the factors that contributed to the politicisation of Irish Catholics. And although Irish Jacobitism never did produce open rebellion, it did cultivate a language and a symbolism of revolt, a corrosive subversive

idiom which could transcend its particular origins and through which later happenings could be mediated.[6]

It must surely be the case that the arrival of the French Fleet into Bantry Bay in 1796 was an event whose meaning was mediated in a major way for the greater part of the local population by a receptivity of expectation and of hope that was founded on both a sense of Jacobite deliverance and a sense of civil emancipation that we can associate equally with the female figure of Aoibheall in Brian Merriman's poem and the female figure of the Marianne in the contemporary popular cultural traditions of France.

I HAVE REFERRED TO THE comparative absence of the memory of the events of Christmas 1796 in the folklore materials collected under the auspices of the Irish Folklore Commission in the earlier part of this century. Two texts of the legend of the French in the Bay do turn up in the Main Collection of the Commission's Archive. An examination of these may suggest a reason for the relative absence of any substantial memory of the powerful responses which the events of 1796 must have evoked on the lines I have outlined in the ranks of the bearers of popular culture and oral tradition of the time.

The two texts I refer to are evidence that in the course of the nineteenth century, with the extension of ecclesiastical control and the spread of the values of a conservative Catholicism into most areas of popular culture, the story of the failure of the French expeditionary force at Bantry Bay 1796 was retold as the story of the victory of the Priest over the Forces of Evil. This story, signifying the historical displacement of the native ancestral religious sensibility by Christianity, has been a major item of both literary and oral narrative tradition in Ireland since early medieval times. The famous ninth century Lament of the Hag of Béarra gives expression in high poetic fashion to this concept of the Christian displacement of the native religious sensibility, as does a twentieth century legend in the oral narrative repertoire of the Blasket Islands as written down verbatim by Kenneth Jackson, from the rendition of none other than Peig Sayers. In both texts the ideology over which the Christian clerical order is seen as victorious is personified as a female of wanton libidinousness and it does not, I submit, in any way strain our legend texts concerning Bantry 1796 to interpret them as portraying in a general way a similar victory on the part of clerical and patriarchal orthodoxy over the challenge of a foreign and especially a feminist-inclined attempt to introduce emancipatory revolution.[7]

No female of any sort is mentioned in either Bantry text but the use of the motif of the priest reading prayers and manipulating the elements to dispel a threat is one that is traditionally associated with the overcoming by a Christian cleric of an evil woman not only in Irish folklore but in the exempla literature of medieval European Christendom. Certainly I believe that the native audience, so to speak, for these folk legends – down to the 1930s when they were collected by the Folklore Commission – would have readily intuited the female nature of the threat that is warded off by the priest, out of their familiarity with the traditional repertoire of oral narrative legends in which such clerical victories over female challenge are a commonplace. That native audience would also, of course, have first-hand knowledge of other encounters in which the authority of a patriarchal Christian clergy is challenged by powerful female figures: stories about Cailleach Bhéarra herself; stories about wise women; stories about keening women at wakes and funerals who on occasion resisted and even fought back against the individual priests who tried to suppress their activities. With such stories of female-inspired or female-centred challenges to male clerical authority still prominent in the oral narrative repertoire of popular tradition in the earlier part of the twentieth century, we can take it for a certainty that at the end of the eighteenth century the world view finding expression in the folk narratives and the popular culture of the south-western parts of County Cork would have contained a lively sensibility of this cailleach/cleric duality and competition in matters of authority at times of life crisis – at times of birth and at times of death, for example.

What I am suggesting here is that the political and cultural life crisis of the prospective French invasion at Bantry in 1796 would have triggered a reaction among the ordinary Irish population that brought together the traditional millennial idea of the deliverance of the female personification of the Irish nation with a modern, United Irishman radicalism that looked to the French model of the emancipation of men and women, and that connected also with the emergent emancipatory energies and appetites of ordinary men and women – such as those proclaimed by *Aoibheall* in Merriman's 'Midnight Court' and represented in the popular culture of France by the figure of the Marianne.

Let us be clear that the strongest evidence I can put forward for this claim here is the reverse or indirect evidence of the transformation of the later folk memory of the coming of the French force in 1796 into accounts – in the legends of the invasion attempt that survived in the folklore record of a century and more afterwards – of how the French, and the female symbolism inherent in their coming, were repulsed by clerical power and authority.

One of these two folk legends was collected in 1936 from an eighty-seven year old woman in Gortluachrach, Kealkill who was born in 1849. The other was collected from a sixty year old man in West Muskerry who tells a far less locally grounded story of the events of 1796 than the older Kealkill informant. The texts of the legends are given here as they occur in the Irish language in the Irish Folklore Commission Manuscripts.[8] The translation is my own. I give the West Muskerry text first.

Nuair a bhí na Franncaigh ag teacht isteach go Bá Beanntruí do bhí fear áirithe sa tsráid go raibh fhios aige go rabhadar ag teacht. D'innis sé do roinnt daoine go rabhadar chucu agus d'airigh an sagart é. An chéad Domhnach eile agus an sagart ag rá an Aifrinn, d'iompaigh sé tímpeall agus do labhair sé: 'Cá bhfuil an fear a dúirt go raibh na Franncaigh ag teacht?' ar seisean.

'Taim anso,' arsan fear ag éirí as suíochán istigh sa tséipéal.

'An tusa a dúirt go raibh na Franncaigh ag teacht?' ar seisean.

'Is mé, cheana,' arsan fear.

'Cá bhfios duit?' ar seisean, 'go bhfuiltear ag teacht?'

'Is cuma dhuitse sin,' arsan fear eile. 'Tá an t-eolas san agam,' ar seisean, 'agus is cuma d'éinne cá bhfuaireas an t-eolas san.'

'Cathain atá na Franncaigh ag teacht?' arsan sagart.

'B'fhearra dhuit an t-Aifreann a chríochnú,' arsan fear eile, 'beifear chugat sar mbeidh deireadh ráite agat,' ar seisean.

D'iompaigh an sagart isteach agus do chríochnaigh sé an t-Aifreann agus díreach agus é ag rá na bhfocal ba dheireannaí, do ghluais an ráfla go raibh na Franncaigh ag teacht isteach. D'oscail an sagart leabhar áirithe (ní fheadar arbh é leabhar an Aifrinn é nó nárbh é, ach d'oscail sé leabhar éigin). Do léig sé cuid éigin den leabhar agus lena linn sin do tháinig stoirm mhór agus do scaipeadh loingeas na bhFranncach ar an bhfarraige. Do scaipeadh soir siar iad agus do báthadh cuid acu. D'iompaigh tuilleadh acu thar nais agus níor stadadar gur bhaineadar a dtír féin amach.

When the French were coming into Bantry Bay there was a certain man in the town who had knowledge of their coming. He told several people that they were coming and the priest got to hear of it. The next Sunday while the priest was saying Mass he turned around and he spoke: 'Where is the man who said that the French were coming,' he said.

'I'm here,' said the man, standing up in his seat in the chapel.

'Is it you who said that the French were coming,' said the priest.

'I am the very man,' said he.

'How do you know,' said the priest, 'that they are coming?'

'That's all the one to you,' said the other. 'I know that much,' he said, 'and it's all the one to anyone, how I know it or where I got it.'

'When are the French to come?' said the priest.

''T'would be as well for you to finish off Mass,' said the other one, 'they'll be here before you're finished,' said he.

The priest turned back to the altar and he finished Mass and just as he was saying the last words the rumour spread that the French were on their way in.

The priest opened a certain book (I don't rightly know if it was the Mass-Book or not but he opened up some book). He read some part of the book and while he was doing that there came a

134

great storm and the French fleet was scattered about the ocean. They were scattered hither and thither and some of them were drowned. Some more of them turned back and they did not stop until they reached their own country.

The other version of the story, in the Kealkill text, is as follows:

Do bhí sean-fhear thiar ar an gCaol Cill fadó agus saghas seanndraoi a b'eadh é ar shlighe éigin. Bhíodh sé i gcomhnuidhe ag innsinn go dtiocfadh na Franncaig isteach go Beanntraighe. Dubhairt sé leo sa deireadh go rabhadar le teacht agus an lá a thiocfaidís agus gach aon nídh riamh.

Datha Daora a thugadh na daoine ar mo dhuine agus do bhíodh an sagart ag magadh fé agus ag tabhairt fé i gcómhnuidhe.

Lá Nodlag a bhí ann ar aon chuma agus do bhí innste age Datha go mbeadh na Franncaigh chúthu an lá san. Do bhí an sagart ar an altóir ag léigheamh an Aifrinn agus do chas sé thart ar a shálaibh agus ar seisean:

'Cá bhfuil Datha anois,' ar seisean, 'nó an ineosfadh sé dhom cá bhfuil na Franncaig!'

'Cuir dhíot an t-Aifreann ar dtúis,' arsa Datha.

Nuair a bhí an t-Aifreann críochnuighthe ag an sagart ní raibh duine sa tséipéal aige ná raibh in airde ar na cnocáin ag féachaint ar an gcabhlach thiar sa chuan.

Do chuir an sagart mallacht ar na Franncaig annsan agus d'éirig an stoirm a chuir leaghadh cubhar na habhann orthu ins gach treo ach ba mhór a'luach saothair a fuair an sagart. Feircín óir a thug White (an Tighearna Talmhan) dhó agus deirtear gur istigh i dTigh Clarke i mBarrack Street i mBeanntraighe a thug sé dhó é agus dá chomhartha san féin tá rian an fhircín ann fós. Déarfadh daoine leat nár tháinig éinne des na Franncaig i dtír an uair sin ach ní fíor san. Tá sé raidhte gur chuireadar mórán óir i bhfolach ar an dtalamh in áit éigin 'dtaobh abhfas d'Oileán Faoide.

Bhí sean-chrunucacháinín fir thall ansan ar an [?] fadó ar a thugaidís Mícheál a' Chápa. Is cuimhin liom féin é agus níorbh dheallramhthach le haon Éireannach nó Sasanach dá bhfeaca riamh é, ina chuma, 'na chaint ná'n shlighe. Duine des na Franncaig é sin adeirtear. Agus tá fear eile ina bheathaidh thiar taobh le Beanntraighe agus sé ainm atá air na Sullivan Fach. Is minic d'airigheas go mba Fach ab'ainm dá athair agus gur thugadar

135

Sullivans orthu féinig. Dar ndóigh bhí seó díobh ann ach do shéanadar a n-ainm agus ghleacadar sloinne Gaedheal chuchu féin

There was an old man west in Kealkill long ago and he was a kind of wizard, somehow. He was forever telling that the French would come into Bantry. Eventually he announced that they were coming and the day they would arrive and every other last detail. *Datha Daora* (Davy Daora) is what the people called this fellow and the priest used to be making fun of him and giving him a hard time always.

Anyhow it was Christmas Day and Davy had announced that the French would be arriving on that day. The priest was on the altar reading Mass and he wheeled about and he said, 'Where is Davy now,' he says, 'or would he tell me where are the French?'

'Finish off your Mass first,' said Davy. By the time the priest had finished Mass there wasn't one of the people that had been in the Chapel that hadn't gone up onto the hillocks looking at the fleet west in the Bay.

The priest cursed the French then and the storm rose that melted them in every direction like foam on a river. And it was a big reward the priest got for what he did. White (the Landlord) gave him a barrel of gold and it is said that it was inside in Clarke's Shop in Barrack Street, in Bantry, that he gave it to him and there are traces of the barrel left there still.

People will tell you that none of the French came ashore that time but that's not true. It is said that they had a lot of gold in the ground on this side of Whiddy Island.

There was a stooped shrivelled old man living over there long ago that they called Mícheál an Chápa. I remember him myself and he wasn't like any Irishman or Englishman that ever I saw, in his appearance, in his speech or in any way at all. It is said that he was one of the Frenchmen. And there's another man living west near Bantry and the name he has is Sullivan Fach. It's often I heard it said that Fach was his father's name and that they called themselves Sullivans. Of course there was a great number of others of them there, but they denied their name and they took Irish surnames.

IN A SENSE WHAT WE see in those two versions of an early twentieth century folk legend is the waters of the political *status quo* of post-famine Ireland – secular and clerical – closing over the memory of the events of 1796 in Bantry Bay. The political ideologies of Jacobitism and the United Irishmen have disappeared from popular world view. The civil and psychological radicalism of imagination that responded to the emancipatory vision of Merriman's poem has yielded to notions and standards of respectability and caution. The *giolla mear* and the *buachaill bán*, Aoibheall and the Marianne have all alike succumbed to the values and the horizons of the new world order that has established itself in the aftermath of the Great Famine, an event the memory of which in the records of oral tradition is itself distorted equally with the memory of the French in the Bay. Oral tradition continually recasts the past in terms appropriate to prevailing popular values and to the prevailing popular world view. In this, folklore and popular oral tradition are constantly revisionist to a degree way beyond anything that practitioners of history would attempt. The folklore then of an event like the French invasion at Bantry Bay 1796 is as much a record of the interpretation, the transformation, the distortion and the application and reinterpretation of historic facts as it is a record of the events themselves. Much source criticism and contextual analysis must always be brought to bear on oral tradition in this respect. The present essay merely outlines some aspects of the problems to be grappled with in such an exercise.

IRISH POLITICAL BALLADRY

AN AUDIO-VISUAL PRESENTATION

NICHOLAS CAROLAN

The maker of an audio-visual presentation to a historical conference has some advantages, on the day, over those of his colleagues who make verbal presentations, but many disadvan-
tages when it comes to the publication of the conference
papers. The immediacy of sound recordings and pictures en-
ables him to catch up and hold an audience, that a moment ago
was sauntering back from coffee, more quickly than he could
with words, and he joins with the audience as a fellow-observ-
er and fellow-participant in a common experience.[1] His comments need only be nudges towards perceptions which he has
already primed by his selection of sounds and images, and if
the sounds are musical he has recruited to his side a particularly powerful ally. But, when it comes to cold print, the logo-
centric comes into its own, his nudges lack coherence, and the
sensual cognition engendered by the audio-visual is barely
present. Sound and probably colour are gone, the three-foot-
high images of the projection screen have shrunk to a thumb-
nail or to nothing, and the synchronised show is only a memory. You had to be there on the day, just as you have to be there
when they are sung to fully experience the political ballads
which were the subject of this particular presentation.

The Bantry sequence began with a medley of the only
purely instrumental music, the only music without words, that
was played. This comprised six tunes, all long associated with
political ballad texts, and used by Seán Ó Riada as part of his
film scores for the films *Mise Éire* (1959), *Saoirse?* (1960), and *An
Tine Bheo* (1966): 'Róisín Dubh', 'The Croppy Boy', 'Kelly the
Boy from Killane', 'A Nation Once Again', 'Who Fears to Speak
of '98', and 'Step Together'. These made the simple but important point that political balladry has a component – music –

which no other form of verbal political expression has, not oratory, nor essays, nor television interviews, nor oath-swearing, nor cheering. Like balladry, they can all operate to a degree at an emotional, visceral level and at an intellectual level, but ballads seem to have a deeper pull, a longer life, and a more individual existence than other forms of political expression. It is music which infuses, shapes and transforms their texts, and gives them memorable character.

If ballads were considered only as verbal texts or as historical evidence, objection might rightly be made to their often banal or flat or ridiculously inflated language, to their conventionalised characterisation, and to their factual inaccuracies. But to consider them only as verbal texts would of course be to mistake their mode, misunderstand their register, and underestimate them. The fusing of words and music in balladry is something different to the sum of its parts. Ballads have a power, and may contain historical truths and insights – especially psychological truths and insights – not easily found elsewhere. Balladry is a distinct small-scale art-form, with its own conventions, and political balladry is a subset of it, with further subdivisions of oral folk balladry and literate popular balladry. Political ballads formed part of the mental furniture of most of the people who made history, and it partly motivated many of them, even if the singing of political ballads was, in O'Donovan Rossa's opinion, often a substitute for action.[2]

The six tunes also made the point that Irish political balladry is extremely varied. There are obvious aesthetic differences between even those few melodies, and in them we moved through time: from a seventeenth-century love song, 'Róisín Dubh', which later took on a symbolic political meaning, through the 1798 Rebellion, the Young Ireland period, and into the period of the Irish Volunteers in our own century. There is a layering of time in the body of political ballads. In a night's singing session there is a constant switching backward and forward in time, and time is multiformly present.

But political balladry is not just comfortably a thing of the past, and only a subject for scholarly examination; it can be a living genre with virulent contemporary meaning:

Well, there is an old graveyard, it's up Milltown way,
It's full of dead rebels, six feet under the clay;
There's a black taxi service from down in the Falls,
Michael Stone got a ride there for nothing at all.

Chorus
It's Ulster for ever, *No Surrender*'s the cry,
Our Protestant faith, it never will die;
When the Red Hand has triumphed and the rebels all gone,
The name Michael Stone it will live on and on.[3]

Or, on the other killing side:

I was stopped by a soldier, he said 'You are a swine',
He hit me with his rifle and he kicked me in the groin;
I begged and I pleaded, oh my manners were polite,
But all the time I'm thinking of me little armalite.

Chorus
Oh it's down in Bellaghy, it's where I long to be,
Lying in the dark with a Provo company;
A comrade on my left and another one on my right,
And a clip of ammunition for me little armalite.[4]

My rather porridgey title 'Irish Political Balladry' requires
some definition:

'Irish' involves more than the obvious ballads made within the
country in the Irish and English languages. British ballads
from at least the sixteenth century have references to political events in Ireland, and centuries later the Irish in North
America made and sang ballads about their own political
activities such as the Fenian invasion of Canada. And of
course there are ballads about and by the Irish in Britain
and Australia and elsewhere.
'Political' is to be interpreted in the widest sense – events,
political and social movements, personalities, ideologies,
and so on – and at local as well as at national and international levels. In the context of the Bantry conference, the
politics of Irish-French relations and of the late eighteenth

140

century were of particular interest.

'Balladry' is used here not only in the narrow sense of narrative songs which are typically in four-line iambic quatrains, with or without a chorus, but it also includes what common usage includes: political lyrics. So 'balladry' here effectively means just 'songs', of all shapes and sizes, but songs with a vocabulary and a range of ideas and imagery which make them in varying degrees 'popular', widely accessible to a range of people. These political songs have been Green or Orange, fleeting or lasting, descriptive, inspirational, journalistic, propagandistic, religiously sectarian or aimed at communal healing; they have been mournful, bitter, comic, savage, scurrilous and noble, and a thousand other things.

'Irish Political Balladry' is therefore a wide and varied spectrum of material – dauntingly wide and varied, and only possible to sample in the context of a conference presentation.

Strictly speaking, Irish political balladry or song must be coterminous with the human occupation of Ireland, but of course nothing is known of the music or song of almost all of Irish history. The political songs which must always have existed and which must have dealt with events within and between different ethnic and social groupings, and between the inhabitants of the country and outsiders such as the Vikings, are lost to us.

The earliest surviving material that we do have is in the Irish language, and some of the medieval Fenian lays – the *laoithe fiannaíochta* – seem in a sense political in that they have some rudimentary concept of a nation and of others who come from outside that nation and who are a threat to be fought off. But concepts of nationality really began to develop among the Irish in the sixteenth and seventeenth centuries, with the growth of British power, and out of this matrix over the centuries came many political songs.

The large amount of political song which there is in Irish, right up to our own century, is often more local in its concerns than the generality of songs in English. It seems inconceivable therefore that there were no songs written in Irish about the arrival of the French fleet in Bantry Bay in 1796. The thousands who came to the shore to look at it were almost entirely Irish-speaking – even after the Famine 30% of Bantry Parish comprised monoglot Irish speakers.[5] Songmaking with them was a mode of thinking; and they were steeped in Jacobite millenarian song and the expectation of help from abroad. However the closest we can come to Bantry is a song about the French who landed in Co. Mayo in 1798:

An rabh tú 'gCill Ala nó i gCaisleán a' Bharraigh,
Nó'n bhfaca tú'n campa bhí age na Frainncigh? ...

Do bhí mé 'gCill Ala 's i gCaisleán a' Bharraigh,
's do chonnaic mé'n campa bhí age na Frainncigh ...[6]

[Were you in Killala or in Castlebar, or did you see the camp that the French had? ... Yes, I was in Killala and in Castlebar, and I saw the camp that the French had ...]

There are however many Irish-language songs referring to the French and French political philosophy, the well known 'Ó 'Bhean an Tí, Cén Bhuairt Sin Ort?' [Oh woman of the house, what sorrow is it that is on you?], for example, with its exhortations 'Éirigí suas, a thogha na bhfear, is cuirigí píc ar barr gach cleath' [Rise up, oh best of men, and put a spike on the top of every shaft], and 'Cuirigí dlí na Fraince ar bun' [Establish French law]. What the composer's understanding of 'dlí na Fraince' might have been is another matter, and is unlikely to have been identical to that of Tone's French companions.

The earliest known Irish ballad sheet, printed in Dublin in 1626, contains a song 'Mount Taragh's Triumph' which celebrates the accession of Charles I to the throne,[7] and is the first of many examples of political ballads in the English language made by and for the British colony in Ireland. Three or four were composed, for instance, on the affair of Wood's Halfpence (1724). The foundation of the Volunteers in 1779 led to a rash of political songs, although they seem fairly dull things now, very literary and not very song-like. The Defenders and

United Irishmen provoked much better songs. In these latter eighteenth-century productions, the French make the first of their many influential appearances in Irish balladry, their interest to the Irish lying in the belief that 'despotic sway from France is chas'd'.[8]

It has to be mentioned that there is no evidence that 'The Shan Van Vocht' [An tseanbhean bhocht: the poor old woman], which is probably the Irish song first thought of nowadays in connection with the French in Ireland, was contemporary with the events in Bantry Bay in 1796. That is the version which goes:

> The French are on the sea!, says the Shan Van Vocht;
> The French are on the sea!, says the Shan Van Vocht;
> The French are on the sea, they'll be here without delay,
> And the Orange will decay, says the Shan Van Vocht ...
>
> Shall Erin then be free? says the Shan Van Vocht;
> Shall Erin then be free? says the Shan Van Vocht;
> Yes, old Erin shall be free, and we'll plant the laurel tree,
> And we'll call it Liberty, says the Shan Van Vocht.[9]

This was first printed in 1842, in *The Nation* – although it is said to have been in existence before that, possibly in the 1790s – and the allegorical use of an old woman to represent Ireland seems not to be older than the song.[10] It has, nevertheless, had a long life in the ballad repertory, and has been a template for a host of political imitations and parodies through the nineteenth and into the twentieth century.

The impression should not be given, because of the context of this article, that ballads derive their importance from their usefulness as historical sources. This is far from the case. Balladry is a self-contained system. It is an art-form with its own validities – the validities of any art form, and it is simply a separate bonus that it also opens windows on the past.

In conclusion, provoked by the presence of so many professional historians, a mild banner may be raised on behalf of cultural history. The interested bystander to historical studies has seen the study of Irish history widen in the second half of the twentieth century from the history of power to include the history of powerlessness, that is, roughly speaking, from political to social history. There is however an aspect of social history which is still unreasonably neglected: cultural history, to which balladry belongs. Kevin Whelan raised in his lecture a problem of the political song anthology of the 1790s, *Paddy's Resource*: that it was not discovered until recently that later editions are in the Library of Congress and the Boston Public Library. This is absolutely typical of the state of Irish popular culture studies: very poor collection of materials, dreadful bibliography, discography somewhat better, filmography beginning to be addressed, videography untackled, ephemera studies non-existent. If the body of professional historians appreciates to a greater degree the value of cultural materials to their occupation, something positive may be done about laying the library and archival foundations for this study in the next century.

THE IDEA OF A TOWN
IN BANTRY

KEVIN HOURIHAN

This chapter is concerned with the town of Bantry. At present, Bantry is home to some 3,000 people. It has an important economic role, well-developed social amenities, and a strong claim (despite Skibbereen's rivalry) to be recognised as the regional centre of West Cork. Yet it is also the product of some 400 years of history and still shows clearly the effects of many of the influences that shaped it. The purpose of this paper is to explore some of these influences. It will not focus directly on 1796; the French armada was only one brief event in the 400 years, and probably did not leave any significant impact on the town (anyway, reliable data sources on Bantry at that time are quite scarce). Also, I will not examine the town's development in a chronological fashion.

Instead, the themes that will be developed are derived from a book titled *The Idea of a Town: The Anthropology of Urban Form in Rome, Italy and the Ancient World*, which was written by the art historian, Joseph Rykwert, and first published in 1976. The connections between pre-Christian Roman and Etruscan cities in Italy and the town of Bantry might at first glance seem tenuous, but I will argue that there are many parallels and similarities or, at the very least, analogies which apply. The cities and towns of Italy are regarded as being both very beautiful and important milestones of European civilisation, whereas we Irish treat our cities with disinterest, or maybe even distaste. In the words of two historical geographers, we have viewed our towns as 'alien institutions, the last symbolically negative vestige of the island's history of subordination'.[1] I hope that examining the similarities between Bantry and Italian towns will help counter this attitude. Nevertheless, most Irish towns *were* established for colonial purposes, as were most of the Roman and Etruscan cities examined by Rykwert, so that provides a direct parallel. In general, all towns were begun for one or more of a variety of purposes – economic, social, cultural or political – and the same influences helped to shape their growth or decline, whether in Italy or Ireland. Accordingly, I hope that focusing on the main themes in *The Idea of a Town* (to the extent of using the chapter titles as subheadings for the paper) will show the shared heritage of Irish and foreign towns, and will help avoid what has been called the 'insularity of explanation' that has characterised much past research in the urban historical geography of Ireland.[2]

TOWN AND RITE: ROME AND ROMULUS

The legend of Rome's foundation is one of the most attractive in city history. The twin babies, Romulus and Remus were set adrift in a basket on the River Tiber, were washed ashore near the Palatine (one of the seven hills of Rome), suckled by a she-wolf, raised by shepherds, and became the founders of the city. The statue of the infants and the wolf is an enduring symbol of Rome. Later however, Remus was allegedly killed by Romulus. Rykwert comments rather cynically that there was 'nothing unusual about the combination of murderer, fratricide and town founder' and certainly history is replete with cities and towns founded by despots and killers.

For better or worse, Bantry has no direct equivalent to Romulus. No individual has been identified as the town's founding-father, but Pádraig Ó Maidín has argued that a settler named Edward Davenant played an important role in the early seventeenth century.[3] A brother of the bishop of Salisbury, he arrived in Bantry in 1608, aged at least fifty years, after leasing the townlands around the site of the town from Owen O'Sullivan Beare. Davenant was a noted scholar who studied for two or three hours each morning before work, but he was also a very successful businessman. He later lost everything after a run of bad luck, but was so well regarded that his creditors stood by him, and he made another fortune in the pilchard fisheries.

The pilchard, a smaller and rounder member of the herring family, probably deserves to be remembered as Bantry's equivalent of Rome's suckling wolf. It had been an important source of income for the O'Sullivans during the sixteenth century and was the main attraction for the New English settlers about the year 1600. The pilchard fishery was the mainstay of the town's economy throughout the seventeenth century. It was cured in huts known as 'paleis eisc' (fish palaces) and exported to southern Europe. The fisheries failed abruptly in the 1690s. The local people blamed this on the battle in the bay between English and French warships in 1689. By then, though, Bantry was an established market centre and the collapse of the fishery did not lead to the town's demise.

CITY AND SITE

In classical times, the choice of a site was influenced by both practical and ritual considerations. Both Plato and Aristotle made common-sense suggestions for choosing healthy slopes, adapting the layout to the climate and avoiding features like marshes. However, the decisions of the gods were also crucial, with the famous oracle at Delphi, for example, playing an important role, and other auguries and auspices (like the liver and intestines of slaughtered animals) also being consulted.

In the case of Bantry, the choice of a site was not conditioned by such lofty considerations. The main attractions were access to the sea, shelter from the prevailing south-west winds, beaches where the wooden fishing boats could be dragged ashore, and the supply of fresh water from the Mill Stream. As a site for a small fishing settlement in the seventeenth century, it was compact and natural-looking, but it has many limitations for a town in the 1990s. The steep-sided drumlins limit expansion around the old town centre and encourage ribbon development along the main access roads. It is also very difficult to bypass, and traffic congestion can be extremely heavy, especially in the busy summer months.

Yet this site was not inevitable. Within fifty years, Cromwell's son-in-law, Henry Ireton, built a star-shaped fort (which still survives) one mile north of the old town (Ballygubbin as it was then called), and a new town developed around the fort. Petty's *Down Survey* shows both settlements and the 1659 Census lists more people at the new town (about 300, using the usual multiplier) than the old (about 185). However, the new town did not last very long and settlement again concentrated at the older centre. It is interesting to speculate on the relative advantages of the two sites. If the new location had been successful, the growth of the town would have been far less constrained, and the kind of dispersal which has occurred over the past thirty years might not have been as pronounced. Conversely, it is unlikely that the town square would have been as impressive as it presently is.

Along with the site, the traditional geographic influence on the growth of a town is its situation, or location in relation to routeways and transport. At present, Bantry is a natural transport hub, with routeways funnelling towards it from the peninsulas to the west and through the mountain gaps to the north and east. In the early seventeenth century, this was totally different. Frank Mitchell has tried to reconstruct the Tudor view of Ireland from the Pale.[4] The mountains of Wicklow and the west would have looked rebellious and threatening, as would the drumlin belt to the north-west, with its woodlands, lakes, bogs, and sluggish streams. If the Tudors bothered looking towards Bantry, they would have encountered both mountains and drumlins, and dense natural woods covering most of the lowland up to 500 feet: a far from attractive scenario, which may partly explain the relatively slow exploitation of the region. Besides the difficult terrain, the inhabitants were 'one of the great long-lasting outliers of essentially Gaelic culture', according to Smyth, which also impeded its development.[5]

GUARDIANS OF CENTRE, GUARDIANS OF BOUNDARIES
The centres of Roman cities had a variety of guardians. The Vestal virgins, for example, were best-known as the keepers of the sacred flame, but they also held in their treasury sacred objects associated with the city's origins.[6] Although there is no direct analogy in Bantry or other Irish towns, the idea of guardianship does imply control or dominance, which are important factors in understanding the development of most towns.

In this context, the guardians of the Irish plantation towns were of a foreign culture, expressly chosen for their presumed superiority over the natives, although Buchanan has argued that this selection was less rigorous in the plantations of the south than in Ulster.[7] The towns were certainly heterogenetic in that they sprang from a foreign rather than indigenous culture, and it is tempting to label them as economically parasitic rather than generative. The historical geography of the past twenty years, however, would be more cautious on both counts.[8]

Rather than being an exclusively colonial outpost, the 1659 Census shows Bantry's population to have been predominantly Irish. The 'New English' comprised less than one-quarter of the two settlements and the two peoples must have been heavily inter-dependent. In O'Connor's words, the 'cultural strands hung together, hung separately, and inter-acted, one with the other'.[9]

The guardianship of Bantry became more clear-cut in the eighteenth century, with the development of the estates and landlord system. Traditionally, the nationalist viewpoint associated landlordism with extortionate rents, coercion and absenteeism, but in his review of the system, Proudfoot argues for a changing perspective.[10] More recent research has stressed the improvements initiated by most landlords and the constraints under which many of them were operating.

In Bantry's case, there certainly were changes. The woodlands were cleared and furnaces were set up at several locations near trees suitable for charcoal. The deforested land was used for agriculture. With the innovations of the agricultural revolution of the eighteenth century, new crops and rotations were introduced and flax was grown as the basis for linen-weaving, a cottage industry which became quite important around Bantry. In other respects, the improvements were less marked. Smyth has shown that innovations like tree-planting by tenants was more sporadic in Bantry than in the more prosperous parts of the county.[11]

The impact of landlordism on the town itself was less pronounced. Certainly, it never experienced the impressive developments of places like Kenmare and Mitchelstown, or even the smaller scale improvements of towns like Dunmanway and Inishannon. In part, this was probably due to the fact that the Bantry estate, although large, was not very affluent.

In many respects, the most tangible reminder of the land-lord era is Bantry House and demesne. It is an excellent example of the architecture and ornamentation of Irish landlordism, and an important tourist attraction, but it should also be seen as a local expression of the feudal castles, Renaissance chateaux, royal palaces and military citadels which dominate cities and towns across the continent of Europe. They are potent reminders of the ambivalent relationship of the guardians and the common people, on the one hand their benefactors and protectors, but also their superiors, exploiters and oppressors.

By the early nineteenth century, a new guardian was becoming increasingly important. From 1778 onwards, the penal restrictions on Catholics were reduced by parliament, and the state became increasingly active in providing services. Bantry received a police barracks and courthouse, and after the Poor Relief Act of 1838, a medical dispensary was opened and a workhouse designed for 600 people was completed in April, 1845. Despite the restrictions and harshness associated with the latter, its role during the Great Famine was essential. Other social services also were expanding. Cullen has described how 'schoolmasters both created and served the need for literacy' and schools provided several thousand teaching jobs at the end of the eighteenth century.[12] Literacy was essential for commerce as well as the professions. The impact on Bantry was below the national average however, and by 1841 over 41% of males aged five and over were totally illiterate and almost 62% of females. (The corresponding figures for people in the surrounding countryside were 65 and 80.)

After 1854, the state made provision for local guardianship through the Towns Improvement Act although the local government electorate remained very limited until 1898, and for another twenty years after that females had only restricted voting rights. Even now, in 1996, Bantry Town Commissioners are elected and operate under the act of 1854, but the real guardianship of much of the twentieth century has been what Chris Eipper, an Australian anthropologist, has called 'the ruling trinity' – church, state and business.[13]

The 'boundaries' in Rykwert's book were the walls and other markers in Roman cities which were sacred and untouchable. Unlike places like Youghal and Athenry, Bantry never had town walls, but the boundary idea has relevance for the expansion and change in the town's sphere of influence, as a kind of mutual dependency developed between it and the countryside. Marketing was an important early link and by 1680 Bantry was recognised as a market town rather than a village.[14] Travel in the countryside was still difficult and was only eased by the building of roads in the early to mid-eighteenth century. The Ordnance Survey of 1842 shows most of the present road system completed. By then, stage-coaches had been introduced to link the main towns, although the two-horse car running between Bantry and Glengarriff was, according to Thackeray, 'arranged so that you may get as much practice in being wet as possible'.[15] Nevertheless, by the early nineteenth century, the town was the economic and social hub for the surrounding countryside (a fact that was recognised by the Poor Law Union) of over 107,000 acres (167 square miles) centred on Bantry and the later Rural District.

The other direction that Bantry's boundaries were expanding was westwards, to the sea. By the late eighteenth century, the fisheries had revived, no longer for pilchards, but for hake, mackerel, sprat and herrings. Over 1,100 men worked in the Bantry fishing boats in 1821. The port was also involved in exporting the produce of the countryside, mainly butter, meat, flour and corn, and importing tea, sugar, spirits, tobacco, coal and iron. As well as the legitimate imports, brandy and rum were smuggled ashore, according to some contemporary accounts. The dredging of 'coral sand' in the bay was also important. It was carried considerable distances from Bantry for use as agricultural fertiliser in the countryside. This business was carried on until the 1950s, and is commemorated today in the 'sand quays' which still survive at the head of the bay.

Many classical cities were laid out within a square or at least rectilineal framework, and further subdivided by the main streets which intersected at right angles. Other streets too were orthogonal, and the gridiron was also used for the agora, forum, or other public open spaces. Many historians have seen these shapes as the unsophisticated results of basic surveying techniques. In contrast, Rykwert argues that that they derived from conceptual models which reflected divine laws.[16] To him, the gridiron layout (much-maligned during the twentieth century) reflects 'the elaborate geometrical and topological structure of the Roman town growing out of and growing round a system of custom and belief which made it a perfect vehicle for a culture and way of life'.

In contrast, Bantry's street pattern was very much an organic one, which developed gradually in response to population and economic growth and adapted strongly to the steep slopes and rocky outcrops of the site. Many streets twist and turn and even today there are large expanses within the built-up area (like Carraig na gCat) which are too steep for building. The Ordnance Survey of 1842 shows the town in that year (Fig. 1). Street patterns are usually the most unchanging features of a town or city (even when cities have been totally destroyed in wars, the original street layouts have almost always been retained for rebuilding them), and Bantry's streets in 1996 are almost identical to 1842. Undoubtedly, this contributes to traffic congestion at present, but it also provides a continuity with the past (as do the Roman street patterns of Verona, Cologne, York, etc.).

In other respects, fortunately, there is less continuity. Much of the built environment in the 1840s was extremely poor. The 1841 census recorded 613 houses in the town but over three-quarters of these were third- or fourth-class dwellings. These census categories comprised mud cabins or cottages of varying size, but Thackeray left a more realistic description of hovels 'not six feet long or five feet high, built of stones huddled together, a hole being left for the people to creep in at, a ruined thatch to keep out some little portion of the rain'.[17] These have

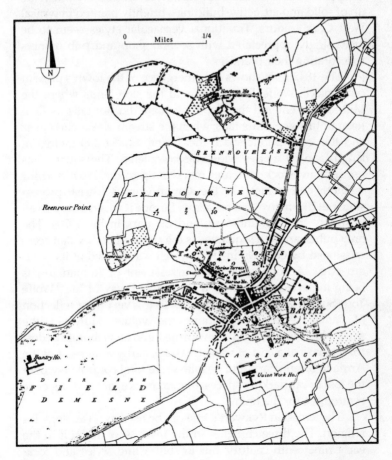

Figure 1 – The first Ordnance Survey map of the town shows the cramped site between the drumlins to the north and south, and the congested streets of the centre. The town square was beginning to develop around the estuary of the Mill Stream, but the Glengarriff Road to the north also shows the start of ribbon development. The seventeenth scentury fort and site of 'Newtown' are in the top centre of the map, while Bantry House and Demesne are in the lower left. The newly-built Union Work House is south of the town above the rocky outcrop of Carrignagat, and further south the land rises steeply to Knocknaveagh (934 feet OD).

Based on the Ordnance Survey by permission of the government (Permit No. 6379).

153

disappeared and for the most part the centre of Bantry is made up of solid and attractive buildings, brightly painted in typical West Cork colours. Traditional vernacular styles seem to be increasingly appreciated with several shop and pub owners redecorating their premises.

The 1842 map shows the emergence of the town's present centrepiece, Wolfe Tone Square, at the slob lands where the Mill Stream entered the sea. The square did not take its final form until some years later when the stream was arched over and the large public space measuring almost 200 metres in length and 60 metres wide was completed. The square was used for livestock fairs and markets up to the 1960s and for religious ceremonies like the annual Corpus Christi procession, but like many squares across Europe it was reduced to an unsightly traffic roundabout and car park in the 1970s. The only public art in the square was the statue of St Brendan commissioned by Gulf Oil in 1968, which was located at its western edge. Apropos Rykwert's assessment of Roman towns being a 'perfect vehicle for a culture and way of life', Wolfe Tone Square was reduced by the 1980s to a very poor reflection of Bantry people's aspirations and values. However, the square has been recently transformed into an elaborate pedestrian piazza at a cost of some £500,000, partly as a result of the Armada bicentenary, and despite some local controversy over the loss of car parking spaces, the square is again a fitting civic centrepiece for the town.

The 'cross' in Rykwert's title can be used as an analogy for religion. The three churches in the town were all built in the early nineteenth century, but in contrasting styles and locations. The Church of Ireland on the north side of the square is in the neo-gothic style favoured by many Protestant congregations at that time, while the Catholic church is neo-classical. Although considered 'workmanlike' by Maurice Craig,[18] it has a dominant location overlooking the town and is a forceful expression of the emerging power of Catholicism in the 1820s. The building of Catholic churches in Irish towns was a crucial development in their ethos and identity. In Jones Hughes's words, they were 'an indication in stone of the forging, for the

first time since the Reformation, of the spiritual link between town and countryside'.[19] Bantry's third church, the Methodist one, no longer has any religious association. It was sold in the 1980s and, in an early example of sensitive conservation and re-use, was converted into doctors' surgeries and offices, without any serious alteration of its external appearance.

THE PARALLELS

Rykwert argues persuasively for many parallels to his conception of Roman towns, with examples ranging from Indian mandalas to American Sioux mythology and the cosmology of the Hausa people in Nigeria. The associated settlement patterns of all these cultures seem to reflect the same universal human instinct.

The instincts that led to the establishment of most Irish towns, including Bantry, were those of colonisation and the exploitation of local resources. When comparing contemporary accounts of Bantry and other towns in Ireland, however, almost all observers comment unfavourably on Bantry. In the 1820s, for example, it seemed 'the abode of poverty and misery ... beset and buried amongst hills that seemed to cover in shame its cabins',[20] and ten years later, it was considered 'singularly remarkable for the excessive dirtiness of its streets, its houses and its people'.[21] Cullen has warned against accepting descriptions by foreign visitors at face value, as many did not appreciate the different value systems operating in Ireland at that time.[22] Despite this, most observers rated the town as one of the poorest they visited, so conditions must have been extremely grim.

For international parallels, French towns may be particularly instructive, especially because of the central theme of this book. Arthur Young recorded his travels through both Ireland and France, but, unfortunately, did not visit Bantry, so a direct comparison is not possible. At present, the historic towns of France, like those of Italy, are regarded as being amongst the most beautiful in Europe, and there are many well-preserved examples which illustrate how a 'French connection' could have affected Ireland. The colonial settlements known as

155

bastides which were established in south-west France in the middle ages took a characteristic form (Fig. 2). They were laid out on a gridiron (like those of the Roman Empire), with a central arcaded square and a surrounding curtain wall. The English also used this pattern for their outposts in Aquitaine and Wales, but with one outstanding exception – Derry in Ulster – it was not employed in the plantations of Ireland.

By the early seventeenth century, when Bantry was being established, the French were using more elaborate models. The town of Charleville, for example, was built on the river Meuse near the present Belgian border, with a very impressive central square, several smaller squares linked up with an orthogonal street pattern and a bastioned fortification system designed to withstand the artillery of the time. The same type of bastions was used in Ireton's fort at Newtown, but on a much smaller scale. In the course of the seventeenth century, the French were the most advanced society in Europe in urban development, with places like Richelieu in the Loire valley where a town was developed by the cardinal of that name to complement his chateau and gardens. On an even grander scale, the palace, gardens and town complex of Versailles was built for Louis XIV, and Sebastien de Vauban was responsible for designing huge numbers of fortified towns on the coastline and borders of the country, culminating in Neuf Brisach in the early eighteenth century. The order and regularity of all these French developments are totally different to the constrained, organic growth that was occurring in Bantry at that time.

Finally, if the armada had succeeded and Ireland had become a protectorate of France, how would this have affected the town of Bantry? In 1796 comprehensive urban planning had not yet been developed in France, or elsewhere, so the immediate impact would most likely have been through fortifications, such as were built by the English on Whiddy Island from 1801 onwards. The outstanding planning achievement of nineteenth century France was the redesign of Paris under the direction of Baron Eugene Haussmann between 1853 and 1870. This involved building great boulevards and avenues (in most cases cutting through the medieval fabric of the city), and

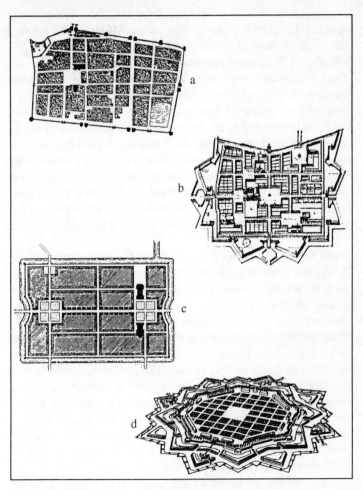

Figure 2 – Bantry in 1842 differs markedly from the planned towns of France, which, under different circumstances, might have been models for it. Aigues Mortes (a) was begun on the Mediterranean coast in 1240, and is representative of the 'bastides', the new towns of the Middle Ages, which were used for colonial purposes in Aquitaine and Wales. Charleville (b) on the Meuse near Belgium was founded in 1608, near the time when Bantry was started. Towns which were developed in conjunction with chateaux were influenced by Richelieu (c) in the Loire Valley, which was laid out in 1631, and Neuf Brisach (d) to the south of Strasbourg represents the culmination of seventeenth century French military fortifications.

opening up public squares and parks. Much of the present grandeur of Paris is due to these developments, but the philosophy of 'Haussmannisation' as it was called, was also applied in smaller French provincial cities and towns, sometimes creating very unsightly effects of wide, straight avenues slicing through old medieval townscapes. The site of Bantry would not have been suitable for these developments, but in a French-inspired Ireland, they could well have been forced through. On the positive side, France was the first country in Europe to list historic monuments for preservation, and since the 1960s especially, French conservation policies in cities and towns have been the most advanced in the world. Historic towns in Ireland would certainly have benefited from this influence.

THE CITY AS A CURABLE DISEASE: RITUAL AND HYSTERIA

Given the scale and nature of the problems which nowadays seem to be concentrated in towns and cities, the continuing relevance of Rykwert's thesis might seem questionable. On the contrary, in the second edition of the book (published by MIT Press in 1988), he argues that it was even more important because of the thoughtless planning and development which had occurred in the post-war period. The philosophy which then prevailed was based on universal solutions and models, which disregarded the past and the uniqueness of different places, and instead reduced everything to issues like traffic flows or economic inputs. The traditions and cultures of towns were irrelevant in this approach, and the built environment had no intrinsic value beyond its practical usefulness.

In contrast, Rykwert's book was a celebration of Italian cities, of the traditions and rituals associated with them, and the continuing identification of their inhabitants with their heritage. Rather than something which was best reduced to a bland mathematical model, Rykwert saw

> the town as a total mnemonic symbol, or at any rate a structured complex of symbols; in which the citizen, through a number of bodily exercises, such as processions, seasonal festivals, sacrifices, identifies himself with his town, with its past and its founders. This apparatus of exercises was, however, not repres-

sive. On the contrary, it seems in some sense conciliatory and integrative, what Freud implies the 'normal' relation should be in this situation.

This paper has argued for the relevance of Rykwert's approach to understanding the town of Bantry. Obviously, the history and heritage of Bantry or other Irish towns are not as rich as those of Rome, but that does not preclude people from the sense of 'identification' described above. Although it will not of itself solve the social or economic problems that are found in cities and towns, it will definitely not exacerbate them; in fact, it may well be the 'normal' relation between people and their home towns, and as such should be valued and encouraged.

As Others Saw Us

Some Travellers' Impressions of Bantry and its Environs

Seán Ó Coileáin

A model for all travellers' tales might be the fourteenth- or fifteenth-century account of an event that is said to have taken place at the great monastery of Clonmacnoise (although another version would place it at Teltown in Co. Meath). In the source from which I take it, Kenneth Jackson's *Celtic Miscellany*, it is entitled 'The Air Ship':

> One day the monks of Clonmacnoise were holding a meeting on the floor of the church, and as they were at their deliberations there they saw a ship sailing over them in the air, going as if it were on the sea. When the crew of the ship saw the meeting and the inhabited place below them, they dropped anchor, and the anchor came right down on to the floor of the church, and the priests seized it. A man came down out of the ship after the anchor, and he was swimming as if he were in the water, till he reached the anchor; and they were dragging him down then. 'For God's sake let me go!' said he, 'for you are drowning me'. Then he left them, swimming in the air as before, taking his anchor with him.[1]

The passage, from the same source, would be transformed by Seamus Heaney in one of the poems in his 'Lightenings' series:

> The annals say: when the monks of Clonmacnoise
> Were all at prayers inside the oratory
> A ship appeared above them in the air.
>
> The anchor dragged along behind so deep
> It hooked itself into the altar rails
> And then, as the big hull rocked to a standstill,
>
> A crewman shinned and grappled down the rope
> And struggled to release it. But in vain.
> 'This man can't bear our life here and will drown,'

The abbot said, 'unless we help him.' So
They did, the freed ship sailed, and the man climbed back
Out of the marvellous as he had known it.[2]

Strictly speaking, although the annals are not altogether above this sort of thing and seem even to make brief mention of this episode, the account itself belongs rather to a standard kind of Irish wonder tale of which there are several medieval catalogues compiled by native and foreigner alike. And the description of the anchor as it 'hooked itself into the altar rails' is more redolent of the equally-distant wonder of a Catholic childhood in Co. Derry than of a medieval monastery. But then, if one may refer by way of analogy to *Sweeney Astray*, his adaptation of the medieval *Buile Shuibhne (The Madness of Sweeney)*, one must always allow for Heaney as well as Sweeney, and one can never be sure which is in the ascendant at any particular point.

As the title of the volume in which the 'Lightenings' series and the poem appear – *Seeing Things* – would suggest it is all a matter of perspective. It is always the marvellous or mundane as we have known it, as we have apprehended it. On the perceiver depends the perceived, not only in its appearance but in its very essence: whether it be air that sustains life or water that extinguishes it; whether one dwells on dry land or on the ocean floor; whether people meet in a church or sail in a ship overhead. The two halves of this upside-down downside-up world are held together only by their contradictory views of one another. When we speak of 'seeing things' we usually mean things that are not there; otherwise there would be little achievement in seeing them and the world of the unseen, lacking a mediator, would lose much of its meaning. But to return to our traveller: he is always the man weighed down by the anchor of his own reality, unable to exchange water for air or air for water, neither here nor there, always desperate to return to his own environment where his miscomprehension becomes comprehension – becomes real once more.

However, although he will not greatly concern us here, we must acknowledge the existence of another kind of traveller, for whom the wonder was nearer to hand and largely to be found within himself. So, Henry David Thoreau could famously write in his *Walden* 'I have travelled a good deal in Concord',[3] a statement that Simon Schama calls a 'wonderful oxymoron'.[4] For Thoreau 'the Concord nights are stranger than the Arabian nights',[5] for he realises, what our travellers generally do not, that 'it is in vain to dream of a wilderness distant from ourselves. There is none such'.[6] Distance was otherwise for him; it was he who required of every writer 'a simple and sincere account of his own life, and not merely what he has heard of other men's lives; some such account as he would send to his kindred from a distant land; for if he has lived sincerely it must have been in a distant land to me'.[7] Such was the variety he found in solitude that he could say: 'I have a great deal of company in my house; especially in the morning, when nobody calls'.[8] This inner certitude is such as to make his situation almost irrelevant, curiously so for one who is forever associated with a particular place, although it might be said that Thoreau rather than Walden is the place where the events of his narrative occur. Rather than being described in terms of his location, the location is seen to depend on him, and he reshapes it as he successively imagines it: 'Wherever I sat, there might I live, and the landscape radiated from me accordingly'.[9]

The Tailor of Gougane Barra, a place that largely remains what Walden must once have been, was much less taken by nature and solitude and accordingly more hospitable, yet he, too, shows some understanding of the distinction when he has one of his characters say to another: '"Travel," said he. "I've travelled more of the world with the light of a penny candle than you have done in all your years of travelling".'[10] We shall return again to Gougane which is, perhaps, best known to literature from Callanan's poem beginning:

> There is a green island in lone Gougane Barra
> Where Allua of songs rushes forth like an arrow.

It was in 1846, in the course of a three-month stay in Bantry with a certain Dr Bourke, who seems to have been almost a patron to him, that Callanan visited Gougane Barra and, it is said, there composed his poem in celebration of the place while sheltering from a thunderstorm, though the reality can hardly have been as simple as that.[11] While born at no great distance from the place, in Cork city or in its neighbourhood, Gougane would have been for Callanan an entirely different world as it was for his fellow Corkman and friend Crofton Croker who tried, with little success, to promote his literary interests; the cultural divide would have been only slightly less had they newly arrived from London, and is certainly sufficiently great to qualify them among our travellers. Compared to Gougane and to what Callanan calls 'the hills of Ivera', wherever he might have supposed these to be, even Bantry would have seemed almost civilised.

Though it excludes native-born travellers (who, however, do not 'migrate interiorly' in the meaning of Thoreau's phrase),[12] such as Croker and Mr and Mrs Samuel Carter Hall, the best general introduction to the historical travel literature remains, to my mind, Constantia Maxwell's *The Stranger in Ireland*.[13] A more curious collection is John P. Harrington's *The English Traveller in Ireland*, a title that rules out some of the more remarkable visitors such as Gerald of Wales (who, to be fair, also falls outside the historical period – the late sixteenth century to the end of the nineteenth – from which his examples are drawn), Don Francisco de Cuellar, Johann Georg Kohl, Le Chevalier de La Tocnaye, Asenath Nicholson, and even Walter Scott.[14] Only slightly less restrictive is the even more recent *Strangers to that Land* (subtitled 'British Perceptions of Ireland from the Reformation to the Famine') whose editors, Andrew Hadfield and John McVeagh, inform us in their preface that, in accordance with the title, 'texts and extracts selected for inclusion here have been limited to first hand descriptions of Ireland by native English, Scottish and Welsh writers'.[15] Finally, I would mention Diarmaid Ó Muirithe's excellent anthology, *A Seat Behind the Coachman*, which as the title indicates concerns itself only with the later period, what might be called the age of Bianconi, since it was he who made possible so much of the travel and therefore of its literature; the book is subtitled

'Travellers in Ireland 1800–1900'.[16] It is mainly with this latter period, particularly with the first half of the nineteenth century, that we shall be concerned here also, principally by reason of the available sources, although these sources coincide only very partially with those used by Ó Muirithe.

The antiquarian fashion of the period has been described as follows by Kevin Danaher: 'Every country man was ready to point out the way to the abbey or the tumulus; every country gentleman had his cabinet of curiosities for the delectation of his guests; every young lady was encouraged to make sketches of ivy-covered towers and romantic moonlit ruins; every rural clergyman could discourse freely on Danes, Druids, Scythians and Phoenicians'.[17] So enamoured was he of such things that Sir John Carr thought nothing of taking two sculptured stones from the archway of a church at Glendalough as a souvenir of his visit, having 'tranquillised' the superior instincts – what Carr calls 'the superstitious veneration' – of his barefoot ragged guide with a payment of money. He comments further that

> The veneration entertained by the peasantry ... for the ruins of castles, monasteries, and chapels is so great, that scarcely any inducement can satisfy the conscience of an Irish labourer to mutilate their remains, even when they are neither useful nor ornamental. This amiable weakness has been singularly protective to the remains of antiquity in Ireland ...[18]

The range of interests of the better sort of traveller may be gathered from this passage taken from Danaher's account of Crofton Croker: 'his cabinet of curiosities, according to the sale catalogue after his death in 1854, held 605 items, the diversity of which embraced a curious double bodied Peruvian bottle, the silver seal of the Cork Orange Lodge, Esquimaux tools, an Irish harp, a mummified alligator, and a cap worn by Charles I at his execution'.[19] Such delights were appreciated all the more keenly for being filtered through a heightened sensibility whose development can be traced in literature from Macpherson, through Gray and Percy, to the Lake School, and in painting from Gainsborough's peasants in landscapes, through the naturalism of Constable's Suffolk scenes, to the alternating poetic tranquillity and awesome grandeur of Turner's creations.

There was nothing in the native literature of the first half of the nineteenth century to contend with this; on the contrary we find its terms of reference being adopted, for example, by Seán Ó Coileáin of Myross in his *Machnamh an Duine Dhoilíosaigh*, 'The Melancholy Man's Meditation',[20] his lament for the ruin of Timoleague Abbey, if 'lament' may be used to describe a kind of nostalgic wallowing that comes close to rejoicing in decay; 'elegy' might be a better word, if only to acknowledge the obvious indebtedness to Gray. As for painting, in so far as it might have emerged in Cork, as in the person of Daniel Maclise, who pictures Croker among the assembled company in his 'Hallow Eve', it would have had to look to London for its very sustenance, not to say advancement; Maclise's friend and once fellow student, the sculptor John Hogan, would make the mistake of returning from Rome to die neglected and impoverished in Dublin. In short, there was no cultural centre that might be expected to hold.

Ireland was comfortably different, not disturbingly so; nor did it seriously challenge the established intellectual or social hierarchy. The traveller, in turn, could afford a characteristic benevolence that tends to find expression in a form of benign, patronising humour, which reflected a tolerance of eccentricity. Eccentricity, of course, depends on where one imagines the centre to be, and for these writers it was invariably somewhere else. (A similar sense of displacement underpins a characteristic Anglo-Irish genre where the essential comic incongruity is supplied by a natural condescension which is as much social as literary; one thinks, in particular, of the writings of Lover and Lever, Somerville and Ross.) Even more than Scotland, Ireland had the advantage of being sufficiently close, yet gratifyingly 'other'; Boswell's comment in the opening chapter of his *Journal of a Tour to the Hebrides with Samuel Johnson* is a fair representation of the underlying attitude: 'to find simplicity and wildness, and all the circumstances of remote time and place, so near to our native great island was an object within the reach of reasonable curiosity'.[21] And, expecting 'to find simplicity and wildness and all the circumstances of remote time and place' with which to contrast, if only unconsciously, the more advanced culture of 'our native great island', such travellers rarely allowed themselves to be disappointed. Expectations were not so much to be confirmed as affirmed, the observation being always subject to the eminently portable governing concept. The compelling argument of Simon Schama's book, *Landscape and Memory*, is that 'Landscapes are culture before they are nature; constructs of the imagination projected onto wood and water and rock'.[22] To paraphrase Thoreau, the wilderness is indeed within ourselves, although perhaps not always in the sense he intended.

If the traveller does not stray far from himself neither can what he writes properly be called literature. Yet it cannot be regarded as altogether factual, for the impetus, as we have seen, is essentially different. While it would now be generally conceded, following Barthes, that all historical fact is finally no more than literary artefact of one kind or another, there are still differences of degree and of category and, being concerned with impressions rather than with documentation, I have chosen the more imaginative accounts. So, for instance, such sources as Charles Smith, *Ancient and Present State of the County and City of Cork* (1750), both editions of Samuel Lewis, *A Topographical Dictionary of Ireland* (1837, 1846), John Windele, *Notices of the City of Cork and its Vicinity; Gougaun Barra, Glengariff and Killarney* (1839), and the numerous editions of *The Post Chaise Companion: or Travellers' Directory through Ireland* are set aside in favour of less factual if not necessarily thereby less informative narratives, although they tend to inform on the narrator as much as on the ostensibly narrated.

Although unable to land in Bantry, Tone himself can be counted among the visitors; indeed his actual predicament of being so near and yet so distant is not unlike that which, in a metaphorical sense, presents itself to all travellers. He records his feelings for the place, or more properly his singular lack of them, although he declares himself capable of other emotions, after three frustrating days in the bay; Bantry, by synecdoche, is now Ireland; with it the enterprise stands or falls:

> I am now so near the shore, that I can in a manner touch the sides
> of Bantry Bay with my right and left hand, yet God knows
> whether I shall ever tread again on Irish ground. There is one
> thing which I am surprised at, which is the extreme *sang-froid*
> with which I view the coast. I expected I should have been vio-
> lently affected, yet I look at it as if it were the coast of Japan; I do
> not, however, love my country the less, for not having romantic
> feelings with regard to her. Another thing, we are now three days
> in Bantry Bay; if we do not land immediately, the enemy will col-
> lect a superior force, and perhaps repay us our victory of Qui-
> beron. In an enterprise like ours, everything depends upon the
> promptitude and audacity of our first movements, and we are
> here, I am sorry to say it, most pitifully languid. It is mortifying,
> but that is too poor a word; I could tear my flesh with rage and
> vexation, but that advances nothing, and so I hold my tongue in
> general, and devour my melancholy as I can. To come so near,
> and then to fail, if we are to fail! And every one aboard seems
> now to have given up all hopes.[23]

But, before going on to consider ourselves as others saw us, it
seems appropriate to give some account of how we saw ourselves, aware that this begs the question of who 'we' are or
might have been and how 'they' might have differed from us.
Something, at least, needs to be said of the Irish language 'we'
(itself a very diverse category), other than that already mentioned concerning the effete nineteenth-century tradition
which, in so far as it speaks at all, seldom speaks for any reality of its own.

'Bantry' derives from an Irish word that would have been
successively written *Benntraige, Beanntraighe, Beanntraí*. The
formation and development is the same as for other tribal
names such as *Múscraige, Músgraighe, Múscraí* ('Muskerry'),
Ciarraige, Ciarraighe, Ciarraí ('Kerry'), *Osraige, Osraighe, Osraí*
('Ossory'). *Benntraige* would originally have denoted both tribe
and territory, meaning the people or petty kingdom of an
eponymous Bennt, the second element of the word being the
noun *ríge* 'kingship'. Alas, of this Bennt, or of his people or
petty kingdom, we know nothing, for the *Benntraige* were an

aithechthuath, a rent-paying or subject people. They do not figure in the annals, we do not have their genealogies, if such ever
existed (which seems improbable in view of their lowly status), and no modern surname traces itself to them; nor can we
say what proportion, if any, of the present population of the
place they comprise. They are known only in the name.

Bantry was far from Clonmacnoise and from its *scriptori-
um,* and we do not think of it, early or late, in terms of high literature. Yet one of the greatest of all Irish poems, ancient or
modern, celebrates this area, the 'Lament of the Old Woman of
Beare', the powerful, disturbing resonances of which even the
mangled text cannot prevent from reaching the modern reader. Much of the imagery is drawn from nature: the changing
seasons, May Day and the onset of winter, sunshine and storm,
growth and decay, and, always in the background as its leit-
motif, the constant ebb and flow of the tide, its emptiness and
fullness. But the *caillech* herself remains the central figure, out
of nature, out of time, knowing that she can no longer defy
them. It has been suggested that the poem originally formed
part of a saga, the prose context being subsequently reduced to
a brief introduction, part of which runs:

> This is why she was called the Old Woman of Beare: she had fifty
> foster children in Beare. She passed into seven periods of youth
> so that every husband used to pass from her to death of old age,
> so that her grandchildren and great-grandchildren were peoples
> and races ... Then age and infirmity came to her and she spoke
> [the poem].[24]

The reference to her seven periods of youth may be based on
the familiar conceit of king and goddess, in accordance with
which the sovereignty in woman's guise weds each successive
ruler and is rejuvenated in him. The Lament may, then, be for
lost royalty: the *caillech*'s final ageing comes about when she
can no longer renew herself in the kingship of her people.
There are reasons for thinking that those people may have
been the *Corcu Loígde,* neighbours of the *Benntraige,* whose territory was originally more or less co-extensive with what
would become the Diocese of Ross. But, like all good allegory,

if allegory it be, it works on an actual as well as on a transferred level, and it is the sense of personal tragedy that gives it
its meaning in either case. On another level still, the poem expresses the chthonic realness of bare, sterile prongs of penin-
sular rock embracing liquid movement and life. Even today, it
is impossible not to be impressed by the suitability of the metaphor of the hag's arms, 'those bony scrawny things', for the
barren landscape. Well might she/it envy the rich lands about
Cashel ('Feven's plain' of the translation) as a hungry West-
Cork hill farmer might eye his counterpart in the Golden Vale.
The following extract is taken from the translation of James
Carney who would date the original to the ninth century.

> The ebbing that has come on me
> is not the ebbing of the sea.
> What knows the sea of grief or pain? –
> Happy tide will flood again.
>
> I am the hag of Buí and Beare –
> the richest cloth I used to wear.
> Now with meanness and with thrift
> I even lack a change of shift ...
>
> These arms, these scrawny things you see,
> scarce merit now their little joy
> when lifted up in blessing
> over sweet student boy.
>
> These arms you see,
> these bony scrawny things,
> had once more loving craft
> embracing kings.
>
> When Maytime comes
> the girls out there are glad,
> and I, old hag, old bones,
> alone am sad.
>
> No wedding wether killed for me,
> an end to all coquetry;
> a pitiful veil I wear
> on thin and faded hair.

Well do I wear
plain veil on faded hair;
many colours I wore
and we feasting before.

Were it not for Feven's plain
I'd envy nothing old;
I have a shroud of aged skin,
Feven's crop is gold.[25]

This is indigenous literature: it speaks for itself, from its own centre.

There is little, to my knowledge, in the later medieval literature that refers to the Bantry area (and one must always be careful to allow that the imaginative location of a piece may be quite different from its place of composition). *Agallamh na Seanórach (The Colloquy with the Ancients)*, which dates from the late twelfth century, reckons among the delicacies of the Fianna 'the fishing of the salty sea from the confines of Dursey and Beare; the *meadhbhán* of crystal-clear Whiddy, *duileasc* from the harbours of Cape Clear'.[26] Interestingly both *meadhbhán* and *duileasc*, which refer to different kinds of edible seaweed, have survived the transition to English, testimony, it would seem, to the more subtle discrimination of the Irish language in what must have been an important dietary area.

Apart from the 'Lament of the Old Woman of Beare', the most moving poem I know from the area is the much later lament for an O'Driscoll chieftain, Diarmaid mac Conchobhair Ó hEidirsceoil, probably composed in the year of his death, 1508. The poet is named as Eoin Másach Ó Maothagáin. ('Másach' was presumably a nickname and means 'big-bottomed'; it goes nicely with the surname which means 'descendant of the little fat fellow', a point that would have been appreciated by Eoin's contemporaries. Ó Maothagáin is now generally anglicised as Meehegan, Mehegan/Mehigan.) While much of the poem consists of the usual catalogue of conventional grieving for a lost patron – the eyes red from weeping, the palms raw from being beaten together in ritual lamentation, the various instances of pathetic fallacy – the sense of personal loss of standing and of patrimony is genuinely affecting. In particular, the image of the poet alone at fairs and taverns throughout West Munster is unusually familiar for the period and suggests something more than standard elegy. This thematic combination of public catastrophe and the poet's private anguish becomes increasingly common in the literature towards the end of the sixteenth century and continues unabated in the seventeenth, no doubt reflecting the social reality of the period.

Farewell to the son of Conchobhar!
It is to me parting with a real friend;
From this death, as is evident,
My eyes I have reddened;
[That] I am without the son of Conchobhar
You may believe from the palms of my hands.

I recognised not this western land;
My honour has been lost;
The death of my kinsman
Is not the loss of a game, but a lasting grief;
It is a sign of Diarmaid's death
That his people have lowered their respect for me ...

It is clear that, on his account,
State and church are equally afflicted;
No blossom in his country is seen,
No day comes on without fierce rain,
The fruit is scarce on account of Conchobhar's son,
And scarce is the milk with milch cows.

No bee requires the watcher's care,
Through heat, in the land of West Munster,
The weather [is gloomy] on account of this one misfortune,
And every person is deeply grieving;
Nor Moon nor Sun shows brilliant disc
After him in the land of West Munster.

Since I heard of the death of my friend –
A disease from which there is no recovery –
Near his grave-stone with torches

171

All assemble in multitudes;
I am alone in West Munster
At fairs and in drinking houses.[27]

Deprived of his livelihood, the poet must abandon the afflicted land of west Munster *(iath/críoch Iarmhumhan)*, leaving the
name of the area to resonate behind him through the poem. We
don't know where he may have turned (if we take it that his
departure is not mere literary posturing), but it may be significant that what appears to be the only surviving copy of the
poem was written in north Connacht for a member of the
O'Duigenan family.

Irish poets tended to be hard-headed businessmen (there
were very few women among them) and were generally prepared to take solace where they could find it. Nevertheless, it
is difficult not to cringe in embarrassment at the spectacle of
Tadhg Ó Dálaigh of Muintir Bháire (the Sheep's Head peninsula) pleading with Sir George Carew to remember the service
paid by his poet ancestors to the Carews back to the time of
Robert, 'the first Carew', a service for which, we are to believe,
the O'Dalys were rewarded by the grant of 'Muintir Bháire of
the sheltered harbours'; now (in 1618), the argument goes, the
land is taxed while originally it was held free. Not surprisingly, Tadhg would have the original situation restored and he
would seem to intend that the arrangement should continue in
perpetuity, a view of things that, in the circumstances of the
early seventeenth century, would appear to be an example
either of severe myopia or of a cynicism rare even among Irish
poets. Or it may simply have been an unwillingness to read
what was clearly written everywhere on the political and cultural landscape from Kinsale to Dunboy:

> Though every *ollamh* thinks that this grant of land we got was
> enormous, we gave your family renown that stayed with [your
> ancestor's] name long after the chanting of [his] eulogies.
>
> Not more enduring has been the grant that Carew gave in
> the first instance than the undying fame that has clung to the
> blood of Carew.
>
> The progenitor from whom you are descended and the

172

ollamh from whom I grew, you and I are their heirs; shall we follow their course?

From your first ancestor, the one who cherished our art, see that we have always loved you greatly; do not abolish my privilege.

The head of my family inherited the calling through which he gained wealth; it is not right that a poet should say to me that I should relinquish this calling.

As I inherited poetry and the wealth it earned from the one from whom I came, I will pass them on to my heir as he [my father] inherited them from our ancestor.

Greatly did our ancestor enhance the repute of your kindred, a reputation that will not be diminished; you were its guarantor when you came with a force for the defence of the Irish.[28]

The idea of Carew coming 'with a force for the defence of the Irish' is not as fantastic as it might at first appear: for instance, several native Munster leaders supported Carew in the Dunboy campaign,[29] among them Owen O'Sullivan of Carriganeas who regarded himself as having been wrongly deprived of the lordship of Beare by his cousin Dónall Cam (Callanan's 'Donal Comm'). Nevertheless, one is reminded of the strictures of Seán O'Faoláin on Aogán Ó Rathaille who, in the poem describing his visit to Caisleán an Tóchair (Castle Togher) near Dunmanway in the early eighteenth century, pretends at first almost to believe that its former owner, Tadhg Mac Cárthaigh an Dúna, is still alive (*'an marbh ba mharbh gur beo do bhí'*) such is the hospitality and joyful celebration that greets him; in accordance with the conceit, he is then informed that the place is now occupied by one Warner (obviously of planter stock), information that Ó Rathaille takes in his poetically mendicant stride, and goes on:

> It is God who has created the whole world,
> And given us one generous man for another who died,
> Who makes gifts to families, scholars, and bards,
> A champion not false, and great of heart.[30]

For some poets, at least, one patron was as good as another, and his origins were no great matter. One wonders what War-

173

ner, and Carew before him, would have made of it all, if it can be assumed that the communication was not altogether one-sided. One is inclined to suspect that Ó Dálaigh and Ó Rathaille were summarily dismissed and told to take their outmoded baggage with them; certainly, whatever the form of words, if any, used in reply, that would have been the practical outcome. This kind of thing is perilously close to self-caricature, as the poets strive to present themselves to outsiders as they would be perceived by them. The caricature itself would inevitably follow.

If we except, as I propose to do, formal historical works such as *Pacata Hibernia*, the first outsider's account of Bantry is that of Captain John Stevens, an ardent supporter of the Jacobite cause and member of a considerable expeditionary force that, having set sail from Brest a week earlier, landed at Bantry on Thursday, 2 May (old style)/12 May (new style), 1689. He describes the place as miserably poor,

> not worthy the name of a town, having not above seven or eight little houses, the rest very mean cottages. The least part of us could not be contained in this place so most were sent two or three miles round to no better cottages to quarter. Two nights that we continued here I walked two miles out of town to lie upon a little dirty straw in a cot or cabin, no better than a hog-sty among near twenty others. The houses and cabins in town were so filled that people lay all over the floors. Some gentlemen I knew who took up their lodging in an old rotten boat that lay near the shore, and there wanted not some who quartered in a sawpit. Meat the country brought in enough, but some had not money to buy, and those who had for want of change had much difficulty to get what they wanted, the people being so extreme poor that they could not give change out of half a crown or a crown, and guineas were carried about the whole day and returned whole. Drink there was none, but just at our landing a very little wort hot from the fire, which nevertheless was soon drunk; and good water was so scarce that I have gone half a mile to drink at a spring. About half a mile from this is the old town of Bantry, much like the new. Upon a hill over the town and creek is a fort built by Cromwell, now gone to decay but never of any considerable strength.[31]

Without attempting to qualify what was undoubtedly an essentially correct response to the circumstances (although it may have been compounded by the conditions endured before landing and, indeed, before embarkation), it is possible that the extreme poverty is overstated in the matter of currency: 'want of change' may be partially explained by the likely persistence of elements of a barter system which Stevens, conditioned to think in terms of so many pence per quart of ale, would not have appreciated. Dunmanway, which was reached two days later, fares no better, although at least it contained 'one gentleman's house'. By comparison with 'the miserable places before mentioned', even Enniskeane is 'a tolerable town' and Bandon, although by this time 'ill-inhabited, many of the richest being fled' due to the general climate of disturbance, 'a considerable walled town, where we found good entertainment'.

There is very little of human interest in Richard Pockocke's account of his visit to Bantry,[32] which deserves notice primarily by reason of its relatively early date: he writes from there on 30 July 1758, having travelled from Baltimore a few days before. The town 'tho' small is the best on the coast to the west of Kingsale. There was a barrack of foot here, now in ruins; & they have a small church & pretty good markets. The Chief support of the town is fish & a clandestine import of French Brandy & rum. They import grain for their own use & have no sort of manufacture'. There is no scarcity of fish, particularly of scallops and oysters; he gives a detailed description of the similarly plentiful pectens, a kind of mollusc, which 'polish to different Shades of yellow, & many in most beautiful reds & white of all Shades'. But the pilchards have already abandoned the bay, and clearly their loss, which would continue to be remarked upon by visitors, was generally regarded as a catastrophe that might, in time, be remedied; in addition to being represented as such, the following has the authentic stamp of folklore: 'Pilchards they had about 20 years ago, & forty years before that, so the common people have a notion, that they will come twenty years hence; whenever they come their ruinous fish palaces will be repair'd'.[33] Pococke also introduces what

175

was to become another staple of travellers' accounts: the remarkable 'coral sand' for which the bay was noted: 'There is a most extraordinary singular thing in this bay, they have banks of what they call coral sand, there is a bed that stretches from the south-west point of Whiddy, & another north-ward from the north east part of it, & there is one in Beerhave[n]. They scoup for it, as they do when they would clean harbours ... This is most excellent Manure for land, & they use it as sand for many purposes; Tho' they take it all away, yet in no long time the bank forms it self again'. He comments on an iron foundry 'carried on to the north of this bay by Mr. White', now abandoned for lack of wood, although another continues to function in the area. He visits 'what they call the Abbey' on Ard na mBráthar, but it is already devoid of any trace of the former friary. It is not an unsympathetic account but neither is it very profound. From one who had spent most of the previous twenty-five years in travelling or writing about his travels in England, Scotland, Europe, Egypt and the Middle East, and who was by this time bishop of Ossory, no less or no more could be expected.

With the exception of Kohl who, remarkably, asserts the contrary, virtually all visitors to Bantry in the first half of the nineteenth century describe it as a miserably wretched place. Typical of such descriptions is that of Thackeray in his *Irish Sketch Book of 1842*:

The town is most picturesquely situated, climbing up a wooded hill, with numbers of neat cottages here and there, an ugly church with an air of pretension, and a large grave Roman Catholic chapel the highest point of the place. The Main Street was as usual thronged with the squatting blue cloaks, carrying on their eager trade of buttermilk, and green apples, and such cheap wares. With the exception of this street and the quay, with their whitewashed and slated houses, it is a town of cabins. The wretchedness of some of them is quite curious: I tried to make a sketch of a row which lean against an old wall, and are built upon a rock that tumbles about in the oddest and most fantastic shapes, with a brawling waterfall dashing down a channel in the midst. These are, it appears, the beggars' houses: any one may build a lodge against that wall, rent-free; and such places were never seen! As for drawing them, it was in vain to try; one might as well make a sketch of a bundle of rags. An ordinary pigsty in England is really more comfortable. Most of them were not six feet long or five feet high, built of stones huddled together, a hole being left for the people to creep in at, a ruined thatch to keep out some little portion of the rain. The occupiers of these places sat at their doors in tolerable contentment, or the children came down and washed their feet in the water. I declare I believe a Hottentot kraal has more comforts in it: even to write of the place makes one unhappy, and the words move slow. But in the midst of all this misery there is an air of actual cheerfulness; and go but a few score yards off, and these wretched hovels lying together look really picturesque and pleasing.[34]

Surely the most fascinating and neglected of all visitors to Ireland is the American, Asenath Nicholson.[35] She must have presented a curious sight, this middle-aged woman approaching fifty, trudging the muddy roads alone, undaunted; with no fixed itinerary except as her enthusiasms took her; only rarely availing herself of Bianconi's 'monopoly', partly due to scarcity of funds, partly to what she regards as its dishonest dealing; laden down by Testaments and Bibles in Irish and English given her for distribution by the Hibernian Bible Society; these she sometimes carried wrapped in a huge black bear muff converted to the purpose since, as an item of apparel, it was scarcely more suited to the Irish weather, even in winter, than the parasol that is blown away in a rush of mountain wind and rain.

Despite such oddities, she is intelligent, of wonderfully generous spirit, and has an engaging self-deprecating wit. The title of the first edition of the account of her travels, *Ireland's Welcome to the Stranger*, seems much more appropriate than that of its later abridgement, *The Bible in Ireland:* the former title gratefully acknowledges the hospitality she received in even the poorest cabins which she, for her part, did not hesitate to enter, while the latter would seem unintentionally to emphasise her proselytising work at the expense of her humanity. She would seem to have been of doubtful orthodoxy: in his introduction to *The Bible in Ireland*, the editor, Alfred T. Sheppard, comments that 'It is a singular fact that nowhere does she give a clue to her own denomination, if, indeed, it had any other member than herself'.[36] One might even question her personal membership, for it is unlikely that it would have been of a strict doctrinal sort.

She arrived in Bantry in late February 1845, having been directed there by Fr Mathew who advised her 'If you wish to seek out the poor, go to Bantry'. In this, he was not mistaken. Mention of the 'African kraal' is reminiscent of Thackeray's 'Hottentot kraal':

> The night was dark and rainy when I reached the town, and a comfortable parlour and cheerful fire hid from my eyes the appalling desolation that brooded without. The morning opened my eyes to look out upon sights which, as I write, flit before me like haggard spectres. I dressed, went forth, and made my way upon the rocks, found upon the sides of them some deplorable cabins, where smoke was issuing from the doors, and looking into one, the sight was appalling. Like an African kraal, the door was so low as to admit only a child of ten or twelve, and at the entrance a woman put out her head, with a dirty cloth about it; a stout pig was taking its breakfast within, and a lesser one stood waiting at a distance. The woman crouched over the busy swine with her feet in the mud, and asked what I wanted?
>
> In truth, for a moment I wanted time to collect myself before I knew what I wanted; at last I told her my errand was to see how they do in Ireland, among the poor. 'An' faith, you see enough of 'em here.' Looking in, I saw a pile of dirty broken straw, which served for a bed for both family and pigs, not a chair, table, or pane of glass, and no spot to sit except upon the straw in one corner, without sitting in mud and manure. On the whole, it was the most revolting picture my eyes ever beheld, and I prayed that they might never behold the like again.[37]

She visits the newly constructed poorhouse, 'certainly the most respectable of any building in Bantry', and regrets 'that the money laid out to build and pay a keeper for sitting alone in the mansion had not been expended in giving work to the starving poor'. She was not to know that there would be use enough for it, and for ancillary buildings, within a very short period. She returns disheartened to her lodgings 'the only oasis in this woe-begone place', and continues:

> The next day found matters no better, and after again wading through a few streets, I returned disgusted at the nausea, which was sickening in the extreme. I left an Irish Testament where the man of the family could read Irish well, and where no Bible had ever been. The peasants in this part of the country are not so afraid of the Scriptures if they speak Irish, because they attach a kind of sanctity to this language.[38]

Attempting to find someone who would help her to carry her belongings as far as Glengarriff (finally settling for the 'John' of a later passage) she comes on what she calls 'Wigwam Row'; the implied comparison of the condition of the Irish with that of the native Americans was not new, although here made in reverse by one who had made the journey in the opposite direction:

> This Wigwam Row is entitled to a little explanation. It consists of a row of cabins, built literally upon a rock, upon the sloping side of a hill, where not a vestige of grass can grow, the rock being a continued flat piece like slate. The favoured ones who dwell there pay no rent, having been allowed in the season of the cholera to go up and build these miserable huts, as the air upon the hill was more healthy. And there, like moss, to the rocks have they clung, getting their job when and where they can, to give them their potatoes once in a day, which is the most any of them aspire to in the shortest winter days.[39]

Finally she departs the town, taking the Ballylickey road. What follows is an unusually sophisticated perspective in that much of the description is of the viewer as viewed:

> We soon left sight of Bantry, for mud retarded not my progress, and we hurried on to the no small amazement of all we met, who in multitudes were going to town for market. But the Bay of Bantry – the bay of all bays, stretched out on our left with its islands, and the rugged rocks on our right, so attracted my notice, that what with gaping on either hand, and looking now and then how to avoid the mud, my gallant John would be far

before me. He would often sit down upon a wall, till I was within speaking distance, then giving the wallet a further hitch upon his shoulder, would rise and hasten on, thus not leaving me a moment for rest. At last I contrived to lighten my burden, by taking my huge black muff, which was quite the gaze of men and women, as well as the fright of all the children, in mountain and glen, and drawing it up closely at one end, so that the Irish Testaments that were in it could ride safely, I called to the old man, and begged him to allow me to fasten the muff to his wallet, as the day was getting warm, and it quite impeded my travelling. Hanging at one end, and being large and made of the fur of the black bear of the American forest, it made John an object of still greater interest to the wondering peasantry, who all seemed to be quite acquainted with him. He was born on one of the islands of the bay, and had lived all his days within the sound of its waters. 'And what is this, John? and what sort may the cratur be that's hanging at your back?'[40]

Bantry would remain for her the epitome of human misery. She comments, for instance, on arriving at the outskirts of Galway, that 'the suburbs are wretched in the extreme, and not in all Ireland, Bantry excepted, can there be found more that is forbidding to the eyes of strangers'.[41]

In the late autumn of 1842, J. G. Kohl entered Glengarriff from Kerry by the newly constructed tunnel road, being most favourably impressed on his approach, crossing stray rivulets of sea 'by ivy-mantled bridges'.

The little islands between which the barks of the fishermen were sailing backwards and forwards were also exceedingly pleasing. Some of the steep promontories which jutted out into the sea were covered with potato-gardens to the very summits, whilst others were equally covered with turf. In a little creek we found a boat laden with oysters ...[42]

Even Bantry is 'a pretty little town' although 'there is no scarcity of beggars or of rags'. A feature of his stay was a visit to what he calls 'Bantry Castle' (which I first thought to be a mistranslation, but on consulting the German original found that it has 'das Schloss ... das Bantry-Castle heisst'); possibly influenced by Walter Scott and Thomas Moore, to whom reference is made in close proximity, he seems to think it to be 'very ancient', as castles undoubtedly ought to be, but as this most certainly was not. The owners were absent, although Kohl is careful to add 'that they do not belong to the regular class of absentees, but generally reside here on their charming domains'; it is curious, though, that he should think of them as 'English':

> The housekeeper at first refused to admit us, as his lordship was very particular about his house, and besides, the castle was all papered up. This served to increase my curiosity still more, for I had never yet seen an entire castle wrapped in paper. But having removed the scruples of the housekeeper, and obtained an entrance, we actually found every thing inside, from top to bottom, carefully enveloped in paper, in large sheets of the *Cork Constitution*, the most extensively-circulated newspaper in the south of Ireland. The door-handles, nay, the entire doors, the banisters, all the chairs and tables, the chandeliers, the hangings of the walls, all were thus preserved from the dust or the sun. Even a metal figure of St Patrick himself, a multitude of old metal dishes, which were hanging from the wall beside and around him, were entrusted to the conservative care of the *Cork Constitution*. I would not refrain from inspecting these antique dishes somewhat closely, in spite of the paper for the house-keeper said they were old Spanish articles. The castle, though all very ancient, yet wanted nothing of modern elegance and comfort; for the English alone understand how to unite comfort with antiquity.[43]

As described here by the international traveller, there would seem to be nothing as provincial as the provincial cosmopolitan, assembling little bits of a world in which he can never really share; seen from this perspective, there is very little difference between his almost pathetic collection of exotic odds and ends and the antiquarian's cabinet of curiosities containing such items as those enumerated in Crofton Croker's will. Incidentally, Lord Bantry's tenure is generally praised by visitors of this period (for example, by Lady Chatterton and Henry Inglis),[44] although this is but to be expected, considering their own background, and there are some (such as Archibald Stark and James Johnson)[45] who are more ambivalent in the matter. Inglis states that 'he is universally well spoken of', but who spoke and for whom?

Hardly for Máire Bhuí Ní Laoire or for the folk tradition that kept her songs alive, most notably *Cath Chéim an Fhia* based on a battle that took place at Keamaneigh, near the entrance to Gougane Barra, in 1822 during the so-called 'Tithe War'. It wasn't really a war, and the battle wasn't really a battle but more of a skirmish in which three men died, but for Máire Bhuí and her people it attained heroic dimensions:

Is gairid dúinn go dtáinig lámh láidir ár dtimcheall
Do sheol amach ár ndaoine go fíor-mhoch fí'n gceo,
An Barrach 'na bhumbáille, Bárnet agus Beecher,
Hedges agus Faoitigh is na mílthe eile leo ...[46]

Soon the strong hand came about us
that sent out our people very early into the fog
Barrymore as bum-bailiff, Barnett and Beecher
Hedges and Whites and thousands along with them ...

'Thousands' was something of an exaggeration, but then, as my friend and mentor, John Kelleher, once remarked to me, in accounts of Irish battles the noughts tend to represent exclamation marks rather than any attempt at precise enumeration. At any rate, it was clear where the Whites of Bantry House stood in this scheme of things.

It was the world of Máire Bhuí rather than the world of Bantry House that Crofton Croker sought to enter, and Gougane Barra rather than Bantry would have still remained the cultural and psychic centre for most people of the area. Described by Walter Scott as 'little as a dwarf, keen-eyed as a hawk, and of easy prepossessing manners, something like Tom Moore',[47] Croker first visited Gougane in the summer of 1813 'to visit what is called the *"Pattern"*, held on St John's eve, when many thousands of the peasantry usually assembled there for purposes of piety and mirth, penance and transgression'. He was then only fifteen years old and, as he tells us, 'ignorant of the Irish language', but his twice-related recollection of the event easily surpasses any other account, and alone allows us to reconstruct the scene.[48] He describes how, with the coming of night, bonfires lighted early in the evening blazed on the surrounding mountains and 'reflected in the dark bosom of the lake' made an impressive sight. Amid the 'confused uproar of prayers and oaths, of sanctity and blasphemy', of infirmity and robust good health, of washing and bathing, piping and dancing, drinking and fighting, 'rebellious songs in the Irish language are loudly vociferated and received with yells of applause'. He has some of these translated for him by an 'old woman, who was a native of Bantry', and whose own nephew had been hanged about fifteen years before for singing a like song, although 'not one quarter so bad'. These, as summarised by Croker, were indeed bad enough, though hardly, one would have thought, a hanging matter:

> Poor old King George was execrated without mercy; curses were also dealt out wholesale to the Saxon oppressors of Banna the blessed (an allegorical name for Ireland); Buonaparte's achievements were extolled, and Irishmen were called upon to follow the example of France.[49]

This passage gives us a fair idea of popular sentiment in the area in the wake of 1796 (for the events of 1798 would largely have passed it by and Emmet's rebellion caused scarcely a ripple), but as a moment's consideration of, say, Hyde's *Love Songs of Connacht* will establish, sentiment does not guarantee any further reality and can, indeed, function as a substitute for it.

From another old woman who was present, the mother of the boy who had been hanged, Croker noted a translation of some verses of a keen, an extemporaneous oral lament, she had composed for her son. This was to lead him to seek out other keening women, and to record (albeit in translation of doubtful accuracy) some of their compositions which are otherwise irretrievably lost, since the planes of the oral and the written do not readily intersect; when they do, the impetus generally comes from outside the culture rather than from within it, and Croker was very much an outsider. Because of his 'living at the time in a comparatively civilised district', he did not succeed in finding a professional keener until May

1818, and then from the same general area as before.

> This woman, whose name was Harrington, had come from the
> south-west part of the county of Cork. She led a wandering kind
> of life, travelling from cabin to cabin about the county, and
> though, in fact, subsisting upon charity, found everywhere not
> merely a welcome, but had numerous invitations, on account of
> the vast store of Irish verses she had collected, and could repeat.[50]

Following a long absence in London, where he worked as clerk
in the Admiralty, Croker returned to Ireland in 1825 to discov-
er that Mrs. Harrington had died in the interval. A meeting
with Mrs Leary, who had keened her at her funeral, was not
achieved until 1829, 'when upon paying her travelling expens-
es from Bantry to Cork, and promising her a new shawl, she
was induced to attend him, and to recite keens and "old talk"
for him'.[51] Croker's description of the bearing and manner of
composition of these two women provides us with an invaluable context for our understanding of the keening process. But
the context lacks an adequate text, and for this we must look
elsewhere, principally to another Mrs Leary, *née* Eibhlín Dubh
Ní Chonaill, whose lament for her slain young husband in
1773 was acknowledged, even by contemporaries, to be the
finest of its genre. Even when experienced coldly on the printed page, and more usually than not in English translation, her
verses serve as reminder of the great gulf that is fixed between
us and the imaginative world from which they derive. Here
we, no less than earlier travellers, are destined to be forever
outsiders, telling of our encounters with a culture that must
still remain utterly foreign to us.[52]

NOTES

ANATOMY OF A FAILURE

1: G. Escande, *Hoche en Irlande 1795–1798. D'Aprés des documents inédits,* Paris,1888, pp. 4–5; see also H. Calkin, 'Les Invasions de l'Irlande pendant la Révolution française, *Carnets de la Sabretache,* vol. 4 (1955), pp. 60–80

2: Rousselin, *La Vie de Lazare Hoche, général des armées de la république,* 2 vols., Paris 1798, vol.1, pp. 267ff.

3: Archives Nationales, AFIII 186b dossier 860, pièce 1.

4: E. Desbrière, *Projets et tentatives de débarquement aux îles britanniques,* 4 vols, Paris 1900–2 vol.1, pp. 61–7.

5: Marianne Elliott, *Partners in Revolution: The United Irishmen and France,* New Haven & London 1982, chapt. 4. Chapters 21–25 of the same author's *Wolfe Tone: Prophet of Irish Independence,* New Haven & London 1989, provide a superb analysis of Tone's involvement in the whole expedition.

6: Archives Nationales AF IV 1597; Desbrière, vol. 1, pp. 107–8.

7: For Carnot's admiration of Hoche, see *Mémoires sur Carnot par son fils,* 2 vols, Paris 1865, ii, pp. 79–80.

8: M.-L. Jacotey, *Le Général Hoche, L'Ange botté dans la tourmente révolutionnaire,* Langres 1994.

9: There are several excellent accounts of the expedition. In addition to Elliott's *Wolfe Tone* and *Partners in Revolution* cited above, see Desbrière, *Projets et tentatives,* vol. 1, chapt. 4; E. Guillon, *La France et l'Irlande pendant la révolution. Hoche et Humbert,* Paris 1888, pp. 246ff.; E. H. Stuart Jones, *An Invasion that Failed,* Oxford 1950. For first hand printed accounts, see *Mémoire du général Bigarré. Aide de Camp du Roi Joseph 1775–1813,* Paris, n.d., pp. 56–70; *Mémoires du Maréchal Grouchy,* 5 vols, Paris 1873, vol. 1, pp. 263ff.

10: See Guillon, *La France et l'Irlande,* pp. 193–6; F.-A. Aulard, *Paris sous la réaction thermidorienne et sous le Directoire,* 5 vols, Paris 1898–1902, vol. ii, pp. 140–4, 660–2, 688–9.

11: A. Rousselin, *Vie de Lazare Hoche,* vol. 1, pp. 267–303.

12: Archives Nationales, AFIII 186b dossier 859, pièce 58.

13: Pamela Horn, *The Last Invasion of Britain: Fishguard 1797,* Fishguard 1980.

THE WEATHER AND POLITICAL DESTINY

1: O'Brien R. B. (ed.), *The Autobiography of Theobald Wolfe Tone 1763–1798,* London 1893.

2:   Tyrrell, J. G., 'Paraclimatic Statistics and the Study of Climate Change: The Case of the Cork Region in the 1750s', *Climatic Change*, 1995, pp. 29– 43.

3:   O'Brien, (ed.), *The Autobiography of Theobald Wolfe Tone.*

4:   Armagh Observatory, *Weather Register for December 1796.* Unpublished; Armagh Observatory, *Weather Register for January 1797.* Unpublished.

5:   Kirwan, R., *Synoptical View of the Weather at Dublin in the Year 1796,* Transactions of the Royal Irish Academy, vi, 309–312 [1797a]; Kirwan, R, *Synoptical View of the Weather at Dublin in the Year 1797,* Transactions of the Royal Irish Academy, vi, 435 [1797b].

6:   Kington, J., *The Weather Journals of a Rutland Squire: Thomas Barker of Lyndon Hall,* Oakham, 1988a.

7:   Mossman, R. C., *The Meteorology of Edinburgh Part I,* Transactions of the Royal Society, Edinburgh, 1896, vol. 38, 681–755; Mossman R. C., *The Meteorology of Edinburgh Part II,* Transactions of the Royal Society, Edinburgh, 1897, vol. 39, 63–207.

8:   Rohan, P. K., *The Climate of Ireland,* Dublin 1975.

9:   Jenkins, E. H., *A History of the French Navy,* MacDonald and Jane's 1973.

10: [ADM Admiralty In-Letters, with separate file reference numbers, Public Record Office, Kew, UK] ADM 1/613, Kingsmill to Admiralty, 12 and 13 December 1796.

11: ADM 1/614 Kingsmill to Admiralty, 2 and 3 January 1797.

12: Bradley, P. B., *Bantry Bay: Ireland in the Days of Napoleon and Wolfe Tone,* Williams and Norgate, London 1931.

13: ADM 1/613 Kingsmill to Admiralty, 23 December.

14: ADM 1/613 Kingsmill to Admiralty, 26 December 1285.

15: ADM 1/613 Pulling to Kingsmill, 25 December.

16: Jenkins, *A History of the French Navy.*

17: ADM 1/284 Kingsmill to Admiralty, 25 December.

18: ADM 1/285, 288, L. 287 Kingsmill to Admiralty, 26 December.

19: Tuckey, F. H., *Cork Remembrancer* [1837], republished Cork 1980.

20: ADM 1/L287 Olphinstow to Kingsmill, Kingsmill to Admiralty, 30 December.

21: ADM 1/614 Kingsmill to Admiralty, 3 January 1797.

22: ADM 1/L287 Kingsmill to Admiralty, 31 December.

23: ADM 1/614 Lieutenant Gerard Gribbon to Admiral Kingsmill, 1, 2 and 3 January 1797

24: ADM 1/614 Kingsmill to Admiralty, 5 January 1797.

25: ADM 1/614 Captain Herbert to Admiral Kingsmill, 3 January 1797.

26: Kington, J., *The Weather Journals of a Rutland Squire: Thomas Barker of Lyndon Hall*, Oakham, 1988b.

27: Lamb, H. H., *Climate, History and the Modern World*, London 1982.

28: Manley, G., 'Central England Temperatures: Monthly Means 1659 to 1973', *Quarterly Journal of the Royal Meteorological Society*, 1974, pp. 389–405.

'THE INVASION THAT NEVER WAS'

1: For details and supporting references, see my chapter: 'Defence, Counter-Insurgency and Rebellion: Ireland 1793–1803' in T. Bartlett and K. Jeffery (ed), *A Military History of Ireland*, Cambridge 1996, pp. 247–93.

2: See Thomas Bartlett, 'Defenders and Defenderism in 1795' in *Irish Historical Studies*, 24 (1984–5), pp. 373–94; James Smyth, *Men of No Property: Popular Politicisation in Ireland in the 1790s*, London 1992.

3: See the recent fine study by Nancy Curtin, *The United Irishmen*, Oxford 1994.

4: For the United Irishmen involvement in France see the now classic, Marianne Elliott, *Partners in Revolution: the United Irishmen and France*, New Haven and London 1982.

5: See the valuable survey of French invasion projects in M. de la Poer Beresford, *Ireland in French Strategy, 1691–1789*, M. Litt., TCD, 1975.

6: For an important reassessment of the French navy under the Revolution, see W. J. Cormack, *Revolution and Political Conflict in the French Navy, 1789–94*, Cambridge 1995.

7: Portland to Camden, 29 November 1796, PRO, 100/62/348–9.

8: For a more detailed discussion of the armed forces of the crown at this time, see Bartlett, 'Defence, counter-insurgency and rebellion' in *A Military History, op. cit.*

9: Dublin Castle had calibrated the position with great precision: 10,000 men could be assembled in 5 days at Cork, 4 days at Limerick and 7 days at Galway: what might have happened in the meantime was a matter for speculation: 'Return of the number of days required to assemble 10,000 troops in the following towns', February 1797: PRO, HO 100/71/100.

10: T. Bartlett, 'Indiscipline and disaffection in the armed forces in Ireland in the 1790s' in P. J. Corish (ed), *Rebels, Radicals and Establishments*, Belfast 1985, pp. 115–34.

11: Above, pp. 9–24.

12: Cited by E. H. Stuart Jones, *An Invasion that failed: The French*

Expedition to Ireland, 1796, Oxford 1950, p. 147: for weather conditions generally see the chapter by John Tyrell, pp. 24–47.

13: This account is drawn from Stuart Jones, *An Invasion that failed*; P. B. Bradley, *Bantry Bay: Ireland in the days of Napoleon and Wolfe Tone*, London 1931; and 'Narrative of the proceedings of the Squadron under the respective commands of Vice-Admiral Colpoys and Admiral Lord Bridport', 12 January 1797, Kent Archives Office [KAO] Pratt Papers, U840/0170/18.

14: Captain Elphinstone, on board the *Monarch*, Cork Harbour, to Camden, Dublin Castle, 30 December 1796, KAO U840/0170.

15: Vallancey to Abercorn, 19 January 1797, PRONI, T2541/1C5/4.

16: H. Montgomery Hyde, *The Rise of Castlereagh*, London 1933, pp. 171–4.

17: Thomas Pelham to Duke of York, 4 January 1797 in J. T. Gilbert (ed), *Documents relating to Ireland 1795–1804*, Dublin 1893, p. 101.

18: *Ibid.*

19: Clare to Auckland, 2 January 1797, PRONI, T3229/1/11; Camden to Portland, PRO, HO 100/69/62–6.

20: Camden to Portland, 10 January 1797, PRO, HO 100/69/62–6.

21: See the papers in National Archives, Rebellion Papers, 620/26/180, 198 on Cork and Galway's response.

22: Camden to Portland, 3, 10 January 1797, PRO, H O 100/69/23–4, 62–6.

23: Cooke to Auckland, 10 January 1797, PRONI, T3229/2/19.

24: Dalrymple to Pelham, 1 February 1797, KAO, U840/0163/5/2.

25: 'Sketch delivered by Mr Pelham to the Duke of York on the Military State of Ireland' n.d. [early 1797], KAO U840/0189/6.

26: Pelham to Chichester (Sovereign of Belfast), 25 December 1796, National Archives, Dublin, Rebellion Papers, 620/18A/5.

27: Camden to Portland, 8 January 1797, PRO, HO 100/69/7–9; Bartlett, 'Counter-Insurgency', p. 270.

28: Portland to Camden, 2 January 1797, PRO, HO 100/71/3–4.

29: See Bartlett, 'Counter-Insurgency', p. 270

30: Deposition of Joseph Harvey, seaman, 5 January 1797, PRO HO 100/71/39–40: See the printed address 'To the Militia of Ireland' [November 1796] in W. T. W. Tone (ed), *Life of T. W. Tone*, 2 vols, Washington 1826, ii, pp. 325–6.

31: Camden to Portland, 8 March 1797, PR., HO 100/69/128–30.

32: Dundas to Camden, 2 October 1797, PRONI, T2627/4/80.

33: 'Narrative of the proceedings of the Squadron ...', January 1797, KAO, U840/0170/18.

34: P. B. Bradley, *Bantry Bay: Ireland in the Days of Napoleon and Wolfe Tone*, London, 1931, p. 98; Spencer to Camden, 20 January 1797, PRONI, CT2627/4/63.

35: Stuart Jones, *An Invasion that Failed*, pp. 200–201.

'IN THE SERVICE OF THE FRENCH REPUBLIC'?

1: William T. W. Tone (ed.), *Life of Theobald Wolfe Tone written by himself and continued by his son; with his political writings and fragments of his diary*, 2 vols, Washington 1826. Further references to or quotations from this source in the text will be given as *Life*, with the volume and page number.

2: Tom Dunne, *Theobald Wolfe Tone: colonial outsider*, Cork 1982; B. Bradshaw, 'Nationalism and historical scholarship in Ireland', in *Irish Historical Studies*, XXVI, No. 104, November 1989, pp. 324–51; Marianne Elliott, *Wolfe Tone: prophet of Irish independence*, Yale 1989; Thomas Bartlett, 'The burden of the present: Theobald Wolfe Tone, republican and separatist', in D. Dickson, D. Keogh and K. Whelan (eds), *The United Irishmen: republicanism, radicalism and rebellion*, Dublin 1993; P. Mac Aonghusa and L. Ó Réagáin (eds), *The Best of Tone*, Cork 1972; S. Cronin and R. Roche, *Freedom the Wolfe Tone way*, Dublin 1973.

3: *Life*, i, p. 51.

4: Elliott, *Tone*, p. 309.

5: *Life*, ii, pp. 46–7.

6: *Life*, ii, p. 44

7: *Life*, ii, pp. 375–6.

8: *Life*, ii, p. 129.

9: *Life*, ii, pp. 213, 496

10: *Life*, ii, p. 131.

11: *Life*, ii, p. 262.

12: Life, ii, p. 14.

13: *Life*, ii, p. 78.

14: *Life*, ii, pp. 134, 64.

15: *Life*, ii, p. 64.

16: *Life*, ii, pp. 233–4.

17: *Life*, ii, p. 129.

18: *Life*, ii, p. 160.

19: *Life*, ii, p. 94.

20: *Life*, ii, p. 168.

21: *Life*, ii, p. 160.

22: *Life*, ii, p. 250.

23: *Life*, ii, p. 416.

24: *Life,* ii, pp. 422–3.
25: *Life,* ii, pp. 459–60.
26: *Life,* ii, pp. 478–9.
27: *Life,* ii, pp. 491–2.
28: Elliott, *Tone,* pp. 377–379.
29: *Life,* ii, p. 375.
30: *Life,* ii, p. 46.
31: *Life,* ii, pp. 60–61.
32: R. R. Madden, *The United Irishmen: their lives and times,* 2nd series, II, 2 Vols., London 1843, pp. 85–91.
33: *Life,* i, pp. 166 ff., 478 ff.
34: *Life,* ii, p. 379.
35: *Life,* ii, p. 154.
36: *Life,* ii, p. 174.
37: *Life,* ii, p. 215.
38: *Life,* ii, p. 260.
39: *Life,* ii, p. 266.

THE SOUTH MUNSTER REGION IN THE 1790s

1: Quoted in W. J. Smyth, 'Social, economic and landscape transformations in County Cork from the mid-eighteenth to the mid-nineteenth centuries', in Patrick O'Flanagan & Cornelius G. Buttimer, eds., *Cork: History and Society,* Dublin 1993, p. 673.
2: Quoted in Seán Ó Coindealbháin, 'The United Irishmen in County Cork', in the *Journal of the Cork Historical & Archaeological Society,* liii, 1948, p. 115: Ca bhfuilid na Muimhnigh, nu an fior go mairid beo? For the authoritative account of Ó Longáin, see Breandán Ó Conchuir, *Scriobhaithe Chorcaí 1700–1850,* Dublin 1982, pp. 91–133.
3: The best account of the United Irishmen movement in south Munster is still that by Ó Coindealbháin in his series of articles, 'The United Irishmen in County Cork', in the *Journal of the Cork Historical & Archaeological Society,* liii–lvi, 1948–51.
4: This argument is developed further in Dickson, '"Centres of motion": Irish cities and the origin of popular politics', in [Louis Cullen & Louis Bergeron, eds.], *Culture et pratiques politiques en France et en Irlande XVIe–XVIIIe siècle,* Paris n.d. [1989], pp. 101–122.
5: Michael Durie, 'Irish deism and Jefferson's Republic: Denis Driscol in Ireland and America 1793–1810', in *Eire–Ireland,* xv, 4, Winter 1990, pp. 58–61.
6: Durie, 'Irish deism', pp. 56–76.

7: Ó Coindealbháin, 'United Irishmen', in *Journal of the Cork Historical & Archaeological Society*, liv, 1949, pp. 77–8.

8: For Swiney's tentative evidence on this, see Ó Coindealbháin, 'United Irishmen', in *Journal of the Cork Historical & Archaeological Society*, liv, 1949, p. 78.

BANTRY BAY – THE WIDER CONTEXT

1: I. Collins to Shannon, December 1797, Shannon Papers, *PRONI*, D 2707.

2: Lecky, *Ire.*, ii, p. 239.

3: Plowden, *Ire.*, iii, p. 146.

4: *Finn's Leinster Journal*, 30 January –3 February 1796.

5: Cited in M. Wall 'The Whiteboys' in *Catholic Ireland in the eighteenth century*, ed. G. O'Brien, Dublin 1989, p. 102.

6: 'Mallow district in 1775' (contemporary report attr. Rev. James Mockler), in *JCHAS*, xxi (1915), p. 23.

7: *Finn's Leinster Journal*, 9–12 August, 1775.

8: L. Cullen, 'Catholic social classes under the penal laws' in T. Power and K. Whelan (ed.), *Endurance and emergence. Catholics in Ireland in the eighteenth century*, Dublin 1990, pp. 57–84.

9: Colman MacCartaigh, *An am Coga America an uair do éirig na Volunteers ag iarruig free trade*, Burns Library, Boston College.

10: G. Steiner, *In Bluebeard's Castle*, Yale 1971, p. 14.

11: T. Hussey to R. Burke, 28 August 1790, *Burke Corr.*, iv, p. 134.

12: G. Knox to Abercorn, 16 March 1793, Abercorn papers, *PRONI*, T 2541/1B1/4/17.

13: K. Whelan, *The Tree of Liberty. Radicalism, Catholicism and the construction of Irish identity 1760–1830*, Cork 1996.

14: L. Cullen, 'The internal politics of the United Irishmen' in D. Dickson, D. Keogh and K. Whelan (ed.), *The United Irishmen*, Dublin 1993, pp. 176–96.

15: Tone, *Autobiography*, i, p. 456.

16: Whelan, *Tree of Liberty*.

17: Earl of Clare to Camden, 7 September 1796, Camden papers, Kent Record Office, U840/0183/201.

18: E. Cooke to Auckland, 26 November 1796, Auckland transcripts, *PRONI*, T 3229/2/10.

19: J. Beresford to Auckland, 28 January 1797, Auckland transcripts, *PRONI*, T 3229/2/12.

20: H. Grattan, *Parliamentary Debates*, 1797, xvii, p. 874.

21: J. Lees to Auckland, 26 December 1796, Auckland transcripts, *PRONI*, T 3229/2/12.

22: E. Cooke to Auckland, 9 February 1797, Auckland transcripts, *PRONI*, T 3229/2/22.

23: E. Cooke to Auckland, 10 January 1797, Auckland transcripts, T 3229/2/19.

24: Troop dispositions, December 1796, National Archives, Rebellion Papers, 620/34/56.

25: Carhampton to J. Knox, 24 December 1796, NLI, MS 56.

26: G. MacCartney to Dublin Castle, 10 January 1797, National Archives, Rebellion Papers, 620/28/79.

27: Mary Leadbeater (ed.), *Leadbeater papers*, 2 volumes, London 1862, vol i, p. 207.

28: Miles Byrne, *Memoirs*, i, p. 3.

29: Hugh White to W. Barber [February] 1797, H. White to C. Stephenson 13 February 1797, H. White to J. Campbell 14 February 1797, H. White to T. White 15 February 1797, National Archives, Rebellion Papers, 620/28/276.

30: *French fraternity or French protection as promised to Ireland and as experienced by other nations*, Dublin, 12th ed., 1798.

31: T. Graham, 'Dublin in 1798: the key to the planned insurrection' in D. Keogh and N. Furlong (ed.), *The mighty wave. The 1798 rebellion in Wexford*, Dublin 1996, pp. 65–78.

32: [D. Taaffe?], *Observations occassioned by the alarm of an invasion*, Dublin 1796, p. 24.

33: J. Hope, 'Autobiography' in R. Madden, *Antrim and Down in 1798*, Dublin n.d., p. 103.

34: [A. O'Connor?], *General observations on the state of affairs in Ireland and its defence against an union*, Dublin 1797, p. 17.

35: [D. Taaffe?], *The duty of armed citizens at this awful period examined*, Dublin 1797, pp. 4–10.

36: A. O'Connor, *To the free electors of the county of Antrim*, Belfast 1797.

37: C. Warburton to Dublin Castle, 13 April 1797, National Archives, Rebellion Papers, 620/29/243.

38: *A letter to the officers of the army*, Dublin 1797, p. 11.

39: J. Knox to T. Pelham, 16 June 1797, Pelham transcripts, *PRONI*, T 755/5/165.

40: Blayney to Glentworth [June] 1797, National Archives, Rebellion Papers, 620/34/45.

41: H. Grattan to Fitzwilliam, 25 January 1797, NLI, Fitzwilliam MS, mic. 5641.

42: R. O'Beirne to R. Marshall, 3 June 1797, National Archives, Rebellion papers, 620/29/146.

43: *Appeal of the people of Ulster to their countrymen and to the empire at large 14 April 1797*, Belfast 1797.

44: B. Verschoyle to Fitzwilliam, 18 May 1797, National Archives, Pembroke Papers.

45: [J. Sweeney], *Address to the Patriots of Imokilly*, Dublin 1978, [rept.].

46: H. Dorrian, 'Donegal sixty years ago. A true historical narrative,' NLI MS 2047.

'THE FRENCH ARE ON THE SAY'

1: Frank O'Connor, *Leinster, Munster and Connaught*, London, n.d., p. 286.

2: C. J. F. MacCarthy, 'An Antiquary's Notebook 17', *Journal of Cork Historical and Archaeological Society*, vol. 101, , 1996, p. 169.

3: IFC Mss, Vol. 573, pp. 102–3. See Note 8 below.

4: See pp. 85–94.

5: Quoted by Ó Buachalla (*op. cit.*, note 6).

6: 'Irish Jacobite Poetry', Thomas Davis Lecture delivered on Radio Éireann, 22 March 1992 and published in *The Irish Review*, vol. 12 Spring-Summer 1992, pp. 40–49 [quoted with the permission of the editors of the *Irish Review*].

7: The chief female character in the Blasket legend recounts the following incident (my translation):

When I was a young woman, lots of strangers used to come to our house. My father had a pleasure boat and they would often sail in her to one place or another. One fine autumn day myself and another girl got ourselves ready to go with them. There was a young priest in the boat along with us. We had a try at sailing to the Skellig but before we made a landfall there a terrible darkness gathered in the west. My father said it would be best to turn the boat around, but the others wouldn't be satisfied. This dark, black cloud was heading for us together with a gust of wind. The priest looked towards it 'There is some sort of opening in that cloud,' he said. It was heading for us until it was very close to the boat. As soon as it had come alongside the boat what was [to be seen] in the cloud only a woman! The priest stood up quickly, put the stole around his neck and reached for his missal. Then he spoke and he asked her what had made an evil spirit of her.

'I killed someone,' she said.

'That is not what caused your damnation,' said the priest.

'I killed two people'.

'Nor that neither,' said the priest.

'I killed a child that wasn't baptised in my desire to become a priest's spouse'. '

'That is precisely what damned you,' said the priest.

Then he began to read his missal and after a short time she rose up out of the water in a flash of matter and she left our sight.

'We didn't go to the Skellig that day. We returned home; and that is the greatest wonder that I ever saw during my life.'

Taken from 'Ana Ní Áine' as published in Kenneth Jackson, *Scéalta ón mBlascaod*, Dublin, 1938: = *Béaloideas* 8, 1938, pp. 79–81 [published here with the permission of the Head of Department].

8: IFC Mss vol. 536, pp. 100/2; IFC Mss vol. 219, pp. 245–6. These extracts from the Main Collection of manuscripts at the Department of Irish Folklore, UCD, are published here with the permission of the Head of Department. In the case of the West Muskerry Irish text the phonetic spelling and orthography of the original manuscript have been normalised in places.

IRISH POLITICAL BALLADRY

1: The media for this presentation were audio cassette (containing 20 selections) and slides (50), with one song sung by the writer.

2: Quoted in Georges-Denis Zimmerman, *Songs of Irish Rebellion: Political Street Ballads and Rebel Songs 1780–1900*, Dublin 1967, p. 10. Zimmermann's volume is the best single treatment of the English-language political songs. The reader is referred to it for an excellent discussion of all aspects of the songs and their performance, and for an excellent anthology of them.

3: Anon., 'The Ballad of Michael Stone', from audio cassette *The Ballad of Michael Stone*, no publisher [?Belfast], n.d. [c. early 1990s].

4: Anon., 'My Little Armalite', from audio cassette *Roll of Honour. The Irish Brigade Volume 1*, no publisher [?Belfast], n.d. [?c. early 1990s].

5: Máiréad Nic Craith, *Malartú Teanga: An Ghaeilge i gCorcaigh sa Naoú hAois Déag*, Bremen 1993, p. 87.

6: Anon., 'Mise 'gus Tusa', *An Claisceadal* 1, [Colm Ó Lochlainn ed.] Dublin n.d. [c. early 1930s].

7: Hugh Shields, *Narrative Singing in Ireland. Lays, Ballads, Come-All-Yes and Other Songs*, Dublin 1993, p. 43.

8: A line from 'Plant, Plant the Tree', see Zimmermann, *op. cit.*, pp. 127–9.

9: Zimmermann, *op. cit.*, p. 133.

10: *Ibid.*, pp. 56 and 133–7.

1: Graham, B. J. and L. J. Proudfoot (eds.), *An Historical Geography of Ireland*, London 1993, p. 14.

2: *Ibid.*, p. 4.

3: Ó Maidín, P., 'Bantry, origins of an old Co. Cork town', *Cork Examiner*, 20 November 1980.

4: Mitchell, F., *The Irish Landscape*, London 1976, p. 192.

5: Smyth, W. J., 'Social, economic and landscape transformations in County Cork from the mid-eighteenth to the mid-nineteenth century' in P. O'Flanagan and N. Buttimer (eds), *Cork: History and Society*, Dublin 1993, p. 658.

6: Rykwert, J., *The Idea of a Town*, London 1976, p. 101.

7: Buchanan, R. H., Towns and plantations, 1500-1700' in W. Nolan (ed.), *The Shaping of Ireland*, Cork 1986, pp. 84–98.

8: Graham and Proudfoot (eds.), *op. cit*.

9: O'Connor, P. J., 'The maturation of town and village life in County Limerick 1700–1900', in W. J. Smyth and K. Whelan (eds.), *Common Ground: Essays in the Historical Geography of Ireland*, Cork 1987, pp. 149–172.

10: Proudfoot, L. J., 'Spatial transformation and social agency: property, society and improvement, c. 1700 to 1900' in Graham and Proudfoot (eds.), *op. cit.*, pp. 219–257.

11: Smyth, *op. cit.*

12: Cullen, L. M., *The Emergence of Modern Ireland 1600–1900*, New York 1981, p. 236.

13: Eipper, C., *The Ruling Trinity*, Aldershot 1986.

14: O'Flanagan, P., 'Three hundred years of urban life: villages and towns in County Cork c. 1600–1901', in P. O'Flanagan and N. Buttimer (eds.), *Cork: History and Society*, Dublin 1993, p. 408.

15: Thackeray, W. M., *The Irish Sketch Book*, London, 1843.

16: Rykwert, *The Idea of a Town*, p. 25.

17: Thackeray, *The Irish Sketch Book*.

18: Craig, M., *The Architecture of Ireland*, London 1982.

19: Jones Hughes, T., 'The origin and growth of towns in Ireland', *University Review*, Vol. 2, 1960, pp. 8–15.

20: Otway, C., *Sketches in Ireland*, Dublin, 1827.

21: Binns, J., *The Miseries and Beauties of Ireland*, London 1837.

22: Cullen, L. M., 'Man, landscape and roads: the changing eighteenth century', in W. Nolan (ed.), *The Shaping of Ireland*, Cork 1986, pp. 123–136.

As Others Saw Us

1: Kenneth H. Jackson, *A Celtic Miscellany*, Harmondsworth 1971, p. 165.

2: Seamus Heaney, *Seeing Things*, London 1991, p. 62.

3. Henry David Thoreau, *Walden, or, Life in the Woods*, New York 1960, p. 7.

4: Simon Schama, *Landscape and Memory*, London 1996, p. 576.

5: Quoted by Schama from Thoreau's Journal, *Landscape and Memory*, p. 577.

6: For the reference, see *Landscape and Memory*, pp. 578, 612.

7: *Walden*, p. 7.

8: *Walden*, p. 96.

9: *Walden*, p. 59.

10: Eric Cross, *The Tailor and Ansty*, London 1942, p. 72.

11: The best published treatise on Callanan remains that of B. G. Mac-Carthy in *Studies*, 35, 1946, pp. 215–29, 387–99.

12: Quoted by Schama from Thoreau's Journal, *Landscape and Memory*, p. 577.

13: Constantia Maxwell, *The Stranger in Ireland*, London 1954. For a comprehensive survey of such works, see the review article by C. J. Woods, 'Irish Travel Writings as Source Material' in *Irish Historical Studies*, XXVIII, no. 110, 1992, pp. 171–83.

14: John P. Harrington, *The English Traveller in Ireland*, Wolfhound Press 1991. He is mistaken in describing John Stevens as 'a Williamite soldier' (p. 11) and is scarcely more correct when he cites J. A. Froude as an example of a 'more authoritative' writer than those he includes (p. 23).

15: Andrew Hadfield and John McVeagh, eds., *Strangers to that Land, British Perceptions of Ireland from the Reformation to the Famine*, Ulster Editions and Monographs 5, Gerrards Cross 1994, p. 1.

16: Diarmaid Ó Muirithe, *A Seat behind the Coachman, Travels in Ireland 1800–1900*, Dublin 1972.

17: Thomas Crofton Croker, *Researches in the South of Ireland*, reprint of 1824 edition, Shannon 1969, Introduction, p. vi.

18: John Carr, Esq., *The Stranger in Ireland; or, A Tour in the Southern and Western Parts of that Country, in the Year 1805*, London 1806, p. 187.

19: *Researches in the South of Ireland*, p. vi.

20: Thomas F. O'Rahilly, ed., *Measgra Dánta*, Cork 1927, vol. II, pp. 158–61.

21: Frederick A. Pottle and Charles H. Bennett, eds., *Boswell's Journal of a Tour to the Hebrides with Samuel Johnson, Ll.D., 1773*, Yale

1963, p. 3.

22: *Landscape and Memory*, p. 61.

23: R. Barry O'Brien, ed. *The Autobiography of Theobald Wolfe Tone, 1763–1798*, London [1893], vol. II, p. 168.

24: Gerard Murphy, ed. and trans., 'The Lament of the Old Woman of Beare', *Proceedings of the Royal Irish Academy*, 55 C 4, 1953, p. 84.

25: James Carney, *Medieval Irish Lyrics*, Dublin 1967, pp. 28–41.

26: Whitley Stokes, ed., *Acallamh na Senórach, Irische Texte IV/i*, Leipzig 1900, p. 21, ll. 736–7.

27: Adapted from John O'Donovan, ed., *Miscellany of the Celtic Society*, Dublin 1849, pp. 328–39.

28: Anne O'Sullivan, 'Tadhg O'Daly and Sir George Carew', *Éigse* XIV/i, 1971, pp. 27–38.

29: See, for instance, Matthew J. Byrne, trans. from the Latin of Don Philip O'Sullivan Bear, *Ireland under Elizabeth*, Dublin 1903, pp. 152–3.

30: Patrick S. Dinneen and Tadhg O'Donoghue, eds, *Dánta Aodhagáin Uí Rathaille*, London 1911, p. 37. *Cf.* Seán O'Faoláin, *King of the Beggars*, London 1938, pp. 22–9.

31: Robert H. Murray, *The Journal of John Stevens*, Oxford 1912, p. 45.

32: John McVeigh, ed., *Richard Pockocke's Irish Tours*, Irish Academic Press 1995, pp. 158–60; *cf.* Pádraig Ó Maidín 'Pockocke's Tour of South and South-West Ireland in 1758', *Journal of the Cork Historical and Archaeological Society*, LXIII, No. 198, 1958, pp. 86–8.

33: For a very fine description of a fish palace, see Charles Smith, M.D., *The Ancient and Present State of the County and City of Cork*, edited by Robert Day and W. A. Coppinger, Cork 1893, vol. II, pp. 231–2.

34: William Makepeace Thackeray, *The Irish Sketch Book and Character Sketches*, Boston 1887, pp. 99–100.

35: For a feminist view of her writings, see Margaret Kelleher, 'The Female Gaze: Asenath Nicholson's Famine Narrative' in Chris Morash and Richard Hayes, eds, *'Fearful Realities', New Perspectives on the Famine*, Irish Academic Press 1996, pp. 119–30.

36: Asenath Nicholson, *The Bible in Ireland*, London [1926], Introduction, p. xl.

37: Asenath Nicholson, *Ireland's Welcome to the Stranger*, New York 1847, pp. 275–6.

38: *Ibid.*, pp. 277–8.

39: *Ibid.*, p. 278.

40: *Ibid.*, pp. 279–80.

41: *Ibid.*, p. 178.

42: J. G. Kohl, *Travels in Ireland*, London 1844, p. 151.

43: *Ibid.*, p. 153; *cf.* J.G. Kohl, *Reissen in Irland*, Dresden und Leipzig 1843, p. 326.

44: Lady Chatterton, *Rambles in the South of Ireland during the year 1838*, London 1839, vol. I, pp. 55–6; Henry D. Inglis, *A Journey throughout Ireland during the Spring, Summer and Autumn of 1834*, London 1835, vol. I, pp. 201–3.

45: Archibald G. Stark, *The South of Ireland in 1850*, Dublin 1850, pp. 187–9; James Johnson, M. D., *A Tour in Ireland with Meditations and Reflections*, London 1844, pp. 129–38.

46: An tAthair Donncha Ó Donnchú, MA, eag., *Filíocht Mháire Bhuidhe Ní Laoghaire*, Baile Átha Cliath 1931, p. 56.

47: T. Crofton Croker, *Fairy Legends and Traditions of the South of Ireland*, London n.d., pp. xii.

48: *Researches in the South of Ireland*, pp. 277–82; T. Crofton Croker, *The Keen of the South of Ireland*, London 1844, pp. xviii–xxii. In June 1817, four years after Croker's first visit, the 'pattern' (derived from 'patron') was suppressed and Catholics forbidden to attend under threat of excommunicaton: see, for example, Evelyn Bolster, *A History of the Diocese of Cork from the Penal Era to the Famine*, Cork 1989, pp. 237–40.

49: *The Keen of the South of Ireland*, p. xx.

50: *Ibid.*, p. xxiv.

51: *Ibid.*, p. xxvi.

52: For text and translation, see Seán Ó Tuama and Thomas Kinsella, *An Duanaire 1600–1900: Poems of the Dispossessed*, Dublin 1981, pp. 198–219

Acknowledgement

Extract from Seamus Heaney's *Seeing Things* is used with permission of Faber and Faber Ltd.

THE CONTRIBUTORS

JOHN A. MURPHY
[Editor] Emeritus Professor of Irish History, University College, Cork.

HUGH GOUGH
Lecturer in Modern History, University College, Dublin.

JOHN TYRRELL
Lecturer in Geography, University College, Cork.

THOMAS BARTLETT
Professor of Modern Irish History, University College, Dublin.

TOM DUNNE
Associate Professor of History, University College, Cork.

DAVID DICKSON
Lecturer in Modern History, Trinity College, Dublin.

KEVIN WHELAN
Visiting Professor of History, Notre Dame University, Indiana.

GEARÓID Ó CRUALAOICH
Lecturer in Folklore, University College, Cork.

NICHOLAS CAROLAN
Director, Irish Traditional Music Archive, Dublin

KEVIN HOURIHAN
Lecturer in Geography, University College, Cork.

SEÁN Ó COILEÁIN
Professor of Modern Irish, University College, Cork.

MORE INTERESTING BOOKS

THE COURSE OF IRISH HISTORY

EDITED BY
T. W. MOODY AND F. X. MARTIN

This book provides a rapid short survey, with geographical introduction, of the whole course of Ireland's
history. Based on a series of television programmes, it is
designed to be both popular and authoritative, concise
but comprehensive, highly selective but balanced and
fair-minded, critical but constructive and sympathetic. A
distinctive feature is its wealth of illustrations.

The present edition is a revised and enlarged version
of the original book. New material has been added,
bringing the narrative to the IRA ceasefire of 31 August
1994.

THE GREAT IRISH FAMINE

EDITED BY
CATHAL PÓIRTÉIR

This is the most wide-ranging series of essays ever published on the Great Irish Famine and will prove of lasting interest to the general reader. Leading historians, economists, geographers – from Ireland, Britain and the United States – have assembled the most up-to-date research from a wide spectrum of disciplines, including medicine, folklore and literature, to give the fullest account yet of the background and consequences of the Famine.

THE PATH TO FREEDOM

MICHAEL COLLINS

Many books have been written about the life and death of Michael Collins. *The Path to Freedom* is the only book he wrote himself.

These articles and speeches, first published in 1922, throw light not only on the War of Independence, the Civil War and the foundation of the Free State but on crucial contemporary issues.

> The actions taken indicated an over-keen desire for peace, and although terms of truce were virtually agreed upon, they were abandoned because the British leaders thought their actions indicated weakness, and they consequently decided to insist upon the surrender of our arms. The result was the continuance of the struggle.

Michael Collins on efforts to bring about a truce earlier in 1920.

MICHAEL COLLINS
THE MAN WHO WON THE WAR

T. RYLE DWYER

In formally proposing the adoption of the Anglo-Irish Treaty on 19 December 1921 Arthur Griffith referred to Michael Collins as 'the man who won the war', much to the annoyance of the Defence Minister Cathal Brugha, who questioned whether Collins 'had ever fired a shot at any enemy of Ireland'.

Who was this Michael Collins, and what was his real role in the War of Independence? How was it that two sincere, selfless individuals like Griffith and Brugha, could differ so strongly about him?

This is the story of a charismatic rebel who undermined British morale and inspired Irish people with exploits, both real and imaginary. He co-ordinated the sweeping Sinn Féin election victory of 1918, organised the IRA, set up the first modern intelligence network, masterminded a series of prison escapes and supervised the fundraising to finance the movement.

Collins probably never killed anybody himself, but he did order the deaths of people standing in his way, and even advocated kidnapping an American President. He was the prototype of the urban terrorist and the real architect of the Black and Tan War.

AN INTRODUCTION TO
IRISH HIGH
CROSSES

HILARY RICHARDSON & JOHN SCARRY

The Irish high crosses are the most original and interesting of all the monuments which stud the Irish landscape. They are of international importance in early medieval art. For their period there is little to equal them in the sculpture of western Europe as a whole.

This beautiful book gives basic information about the crosses. A general survey is followed by an inventory to accompany the large collection of photographs which illustrate their variety and richness. In this way readers will readily have at their disposal an extensive range of the images created in stone by sculptors working in Ireland over a thousand years ago.

A HANDBOOK OF
CELTIC ORNAMENT

JOHN G. MERNE

A complete course in the construction and development of Celtic ornament with over 700 illustrations. *A Handbook of Celtic Ornament* takes basic symbols or ideographs and develops them into a systemised method of construction for most forms of Celtic decoration.

Apart from its value as a drawing textbook this book will be of immense valve to all students of Arts and Crafts. The Merne method for the construction and development of Celtic ornament has not been surpassed and this book is a challenge both to the student and the professional artist to take part of our tradition and make it their own, to use, to repeat, but most of all to develop.

IRISH SYMBOLS
OF 3500 BC

N. L. THOMAS

The riddle of the inscriptions at Newgrange, Knowth and other equally ancient Irish sites in the Boyne valley have been partly deciphered at last.

The inscribed passage mound stones tell of pre-historic man's concept of the world; the flat earth with a hemispherical bowl overhead, the sun and the moon circling round.

The legends and myths of Ireland can be directly related to the stone engravings; certain numbers such as nine, eleven, seventeen, twenty-seven and thirty-three are common to both. These numbers have important symbolic meanings as well as their numerical values.

The oldest calender in the history of mankind is portrayed – sixteen months of 22 or 23 days, four weeks of five days each month, eight annual solar and seasonal events. It has been known for some time that the passages into the Newgrange and Knowth mounds are aligned with sunrise and sunset on the solstitial and equinoctial days each year. They are the cornerstones of the sixteen month calender and the eight annual festival days.

The evidence from 3500 BC to 3200 BC precedes British calender building sites at Mount Pleasant 2600 BC and Stonehenge 2000 BC.

IRISH COUNTRY TOWNS

EDITED BY
ANNGRET SIMMS AND J. H. ANDREWS

Country towns are an important aspect of Irish identity, blending place and time in a unique fashion. Their stories reflect the formative periods of town foundation in Ireland: from the Gaelic monastic sites to Anglo-Norman colonial settlements to early modern plantation towns.

The story of each town is given added interest by a town plan and an evocative black-and-white illustration, usually nineteenth-century. The towns included are Kells, Downpatrick, Carrickfergus, Maynooth, Enniscorthy, Bandon, Lurgan, Ennistymon, Castlecomer, Bray, Sligo, Athlone, Dungarvan and Mullingar. A companion volume, *More Irish Country Towns*, includes Kildare, Carlingford, Bangor, Coleraine, Carrickmacross, Tullamore, Monasterevan, Athenry, Tuam, Westport, Roscrea, Cashel, Tralee, Youghal and Wexford.

IRISH CITIES

EDITED BY HOWARD B. CLARKE

This publication draws on the leading experts in history, archaeology and historical geography to examine in detail the development of Belfast, Cork, Derry, Dublin, Galway, Limerick and Waterford. Fifteen essays discuss the early and later periods of development of these cities.

The essays, to accompany a series of Thomas Davis lectures on RTE radio, are illustrative rather than analytical, yet the attentive reader will gain considerable insight into the essence of Irish cities as they have evolved to the present day.